The
MBA
Bootcamp

What Every Manager or Start-up
Must Know

Dr. Gerard L. Danford

What You Will Gain

- Improve your probability of career success (success formula, 8 accelerators, and 4 forms of complexity).
- Enhance your management competences (5 essential management tasks, the innovative mind-set, and tools for decision making).
- Contribute more value in your organization (behavioral economics, drivers of value, and PBF).
- Practical tools (budget allocation, ROI, and digitalization).
- Essential processes (Triple Bottom Line, agile/lean, and internationalization).
- Competing for the Future (agile strategy, six career weapons, and startups 10/90 rule)?
- Practical case examples: Apple, Amazon, Google, Lego, and more...

Why I Created the Mini MBA

Having spent 20 years in business (management consulting), and 20 years teaching on Business Programs in Europe and North America, I can say with confidence that there are just 18 essential concepts which every present and future manager must master. This Mini MBA Bootcamp presents and explains those 18 most essential concepts. Everyone must understand these concepts to increase their chances of success in business. Some of the 18 concepts have stood the test of time, while others are just now emerging on the horizon, because nothing lasts forever.

TABLE OF CONTENTS

INTRODUCTION 6

DRILL 1: THE SUCCESS FORMULA 18

DRILL 2: CHANGE 28

DRILL 3: ORGANIZATION 37

DRILL 4: INNOVATION 46

DRILL 5: MANAGEMENT 57

DRILL 6: DECISION MAKING 67

DRILL 7: ECONOMICS 77

DRILL 8: FINANCE 85

DRILL 9: ACCOUNTING 93

DRILL 10: MARKETING 102

DRILL 11: DIGITAL MARKETING 111

DRILL 12: TECHNOLOGY   120

DRILL 13: SUSTAINABILITY   130

DRILL 14: OPERATIONS   143

DRILL 15: INTERNATIONAL   154

DRILL 16: STRATEGY   173

DRILL 17: CAREER   184

DRILL 18: START-UP   193

FINAL MINI MBA ASSESSMENT   205

Introduction

Why a MBA?

There are differing reasons for completing this Mini MBA including;

- **Career Enhancement**: The Mini MBA is suitable for individuals who have specialized in one field and now wish to broaden their knowledge of business or wish to contribute more to their current employer's purpose.
- **Career Change**: The Mini MBA is suitable for individuals who have already completed an undergraduate degree and now desire to make a career change. That undergraduate degree may have been in the sciences, social sciences or engineering. The Mini MBA is one way to discover new career opportunities.
- **Establish A Business**: The Mini MBA is suitable for individuals who have (or are planning to) establish their own business. Those individuals may be looking for new ideas/insights which will help their startup succeed.
- **Develop Leadership and Influence Skills**: The Mini MBA is suitable for individuals who wish to develop their skills in managing, leading, and influencing others. Furthermore, because the business environment is becoming more complex and ambiguous, managers must learn how to deal with complexity and how to improve problem solving skills.
- **Specialized Knowledge and Skills**: The Mini MBA Bootcamp is not suitable for individuals who wish to develop specialized skills and knowledge (deeper learning), within a specific domain.

The Learning Process

The Mini MBA Bootcamp is structured around six themes which are further divided into subject areas (18 in total). The subject areas have been selected based on the goals of MBA candidates, and the author's 20/20 years of work experience (management consulting and MBA teaching). A great deal of time was spent deciding what content should be included in the Mini MBA. The content selected is considered to provide the best return on investment (ROI) and value for time. Furthermore, the concepts covered are most relevant for the immediate future. As the reader progresses through the Mini MBA content, they will find that the depth and detail of that content increases.

Mini MBA Learning Process

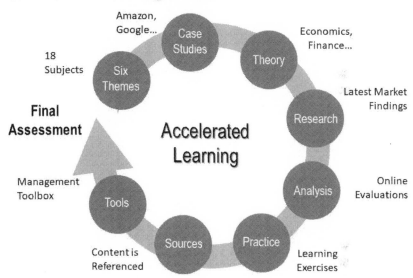

The Mini MBA includes numerous company case studies, which will provide the reader with a practical understanding of the concepts covered. During the case presentations readers are challenged to consider solutions to problems faced by those case companies (Amazon, Google, Lego, Apple, Dunkin Donuts, Santander, Boeing etc.). The Mini MBA also contains exercises, and self-assessment tools. Furthermore, there are links to external assessments which will allow the reader to evaluate their current employer/company, based on the concepts being addressed. Unfortunately, it has not been possible to incorporate synchronous learning into the Mini MBA (interaction with faculty and cohorts).

At the end of the Mini MBA the reader has an opportunity to assess their knowledge of the concepts and tools covered. Completing the final online assessment also allows readers to reinforce their learning and internalize their understanding of the 18 concepts covered.

Overview of 18 Drills

The Success Theme

1. Success

There are two broad dimensions for defining success. The first of those dimensions is external achievement. External achievement is a relative concept, and in fact a person can never get enough of it. One of the many metric for measuring external achievement is money. The Mini MBA reveals the 'Six Rules for Making Lots of Money,' which are based on the experiences of people who have done just that.

The second broad dimension for success is internal happiness. Internal happiness can be measured in many ways. However, one of the most useful metrics for measuring internal happiness, is the satisfaction a person gets after making the right career choices. The Mini MBA presents a 'Career Choice Framework' which can help readers identify the best career choice for their purposes.

Research on the topic of success has also identified the essential ingredients which every person should possess to achieve success (external achievement + internal happiness). A 'Formula for Personal Success' has been identified which is based upon those ingredients. That formula and how to make it work, represents most of the content covered in Drill #1. In addition, the ways to increase ones' chances for success are also covered in this drill. The Drill ends with an online assessment that measures within minutes a person's level of performance on the 'Formula for Personal Success.'

2. Change

Change today is very different from what it looked like 10 or 20 years ago. In today's business environment, continuous and discontinuous change is having an impact on every organization and individual. What this means is that companies must become better at managing change. The need for organizational change is driven by many factors; falling behind the competition, too slow in strategizing, uncertain planning horizons, tactical situations, implementation challenges and the need for rapid innovation. Furthermore, as companies are becoming more and more complex, organizational siloes emerge which prevent them from achieving effective internal collaboration and communication. Change is essential because it serves many purposes; increasing revenues, profits, and effectiveness, along with decreasing costs.

Changing Behavior & Mindset

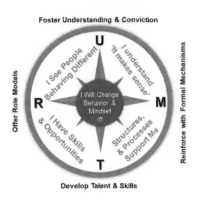

Foster Understanding & Conviction

Offer Role Models

I See People Behaving Differently

It makes sense / I understand

I Will Change Behavior & Mindset if!

I Have Skills & Opportunities

Structures, Processes & Support Me

Reinforce with Formal Mechanisms

Develop Talent & Skills

Failure Happens When We

Assume that 'why change' is clear & fail to communicate the rationale.
Solution: Write A Change Story

Fail to establish associations and reinforce wrong behaviors.
Solution: Clarify the Purpose

Don't instill a sense of control, self-competence & rewards for effort.
Solution: Show Good Examples

Haven't identified and crafted symbols of 'social proof'.
Solution: Small Wins & Achievements

Source: McKinsey & Co.

The biggest barriers to achieving successful organizational and individual change have been identified. Drill #2 introduces 'The 8 Change Accelerators', which help to eliminate organizational and individual barriers to change. The drill ends with an online assessment which evaluates one's capacity for change (strengths and weaknesses).

3. Organization

This Mini MBA drill will focus on: 'How a manager can design and support effective and efficient structures and processes in their organization, to achieve the desired results?' However, the challenge managers' face when dealing with this important issue is that every organization is unique in one way or another. Therefore, all actions taken must reflect the uniqueness of each case.

Bain and Co. have researched complexity in 8,000 global companies and their findings show that every business, almost always, becomes too complex (bureaucracy creeps in). This is important to understand because complexity has an impact on an organizations performance in the short-term and the long-term. Complexity is already an issue for an organization if they are hearing some of the following statements being expressed;

- 'We're losing touch with customers and no longer understand them'.
- 'We're drowning in processes and PowerPoints. Those processes have become more important than the reason we are doing them in the first place'.
- 'We're no longer able to act decisively or precisely'.

This Mini MBA session will explore; the most common causes of complexity and how to reduce complexity. The first step to reducing complexity must begin at the individual level because every employee's behavior and attitude towards complexity, affects the organization in one way or another. The drill ends with an online assessment which evaluates one's behavior and attitude towards complexity.

The Management Theme

4. Innovation

Innovation is a top-three priority for 80% of company leaders today. However, it is important to understand that there are three distinct forms of innovation.

- **Disruptive Innovation**: Contains common off-the-shelf components that are easily available but are assembled together in a new way (simpler than existing approaches or solutions).
- **Sustaining Innovation**: Helps to develop existing markets.
- **Efficiency Innovation**: Reduces the cost of making and distributing existing products and services.

Three actions (drivers) have been identified that turbo-boost a company's level of innovation. Those drivers are; speed, processes, and technology platforms. Each of these drivers will be reviewed in the Mini MBA and applied to an innovation case. The drill ends with an online assessment which evaluates one's attitude towards innovation (five broad categories).

Balanced Innovation

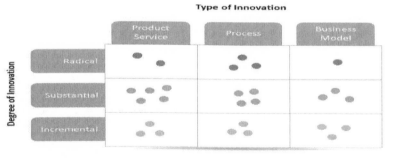

5. Management

This drill concentrates on the primary tasks performed by managers, which help to improve organizational performance. Drill 5 ends with an online leadership traits assessment.

Drucker's' 5 Management Tasks

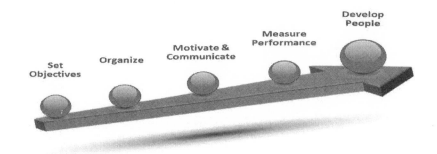

6. Decision Making

Drill #6 covers three tools for making better decisions. The first tool helps to improve time management. The second tool assists in defining the root-cause of problems. The third tool provides a framework for making better business decisions.

The Decision Chain

Each Steps Is Inter-Connected
All 6 issues rank as close to 100% as possible before decision is made.

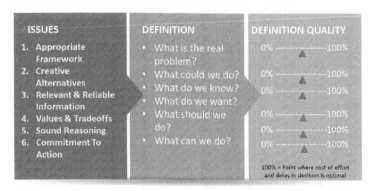

Source: Stanford Strategic Decision & Risk Management

The Money Theme

7. Economics

The Apple iPhone case is used to explain some of the most important economic principles; neo-classical economics, profit maximization, pricing, rationality, and behavioral economics. The drill ends with an online rationality assessment that helps determine which of the 16 reasoning styles a person uses (ID reasoning strengths and areas for improvement).

8. Finance

The Mini MBA finance drill focuses on the concept of shareholder value, which is often misunderstood. The Amazon Marketplace case is used to describe the important role cash flow plays in financial performance and ways to improve value creation are presented.

9. Accounting

The accounting information gathered in a company provides managers with the data needed to effectively operate their business. Furthermore, accounting information can be used to help steer managers in the right direction. Key Performance Indicators (KPI's) are an important tool for measuring the progress made. Therefore, this Mini MBA drill concentrates on how to define the best KPI's for a business. The drill ends with a review of the planning-budgeting-forecasting (PBF) process, and how to improve that process.

The Market Theme

10. Marketing

The hard data which occupy a marketing manager's daily life is the focus for this Mini MBA drill (numbers, budgets, and activities). Topics covered include;
- How to define the marketing budget (level of investment)?
- How and where to spend the marketing budget (allocation)?
- What are the biggest digital marketing challenges and opportunities?
- How to measure and improve marketing ROI?
- What should be the strategic marketing priorities?

11. Digital Marketing

The world has become a mobile-first digital marketplace. However, marketers continue to invest the largest part of their budgets within traditional channels. This Mini MBA digital marketing drill explores; how to assess and improve ROI in digital channels.

12. Technology

Digitalization is also the focus of Drill #12. The Lego Corporation and Amazon Dash Button cases are used to explain how companies can improve their digital IQ. A company Digital IQ can be improved by;

- Developing new and more powerful information analysis and intelligence-range capabilities.
- Defining business processes that support continuous collaboration between employees, suppliers, agents and customers.
- Integrating digital technology into functions that support efficiency.
- Re-imagining the traditional customer-management model, and moving away from transactions, to more individual customer relationships.
- Building and using systems that allow for real-time decision making.

The Process Theme

13. Sustainability

Sustainability is one way for companies to differentiate themselves from the competition. Sustainability can also be used to increase value for customers. This Mini MBA drill describes how any organization can create a 'business case' for a sustainability.

14. Operations

The Lego Operations case is used to describe 'best-in-class' operations capabilities. The drill also introduces research on agility, and the three core capabilities companies need to become more agile;

- **Organizational Structure**: Influences how resources are distributed in a company.
- **Governance**: Determines how decisions are made in a company.

- **Processes**: Decides how things get done, influences performance measurement and accountability.

15.International

The Amazon Marketplaces case study is used to describe the rapidly changing international business environment, and what actions (tools) need to be taken to address these changes. The OLI Framework and IR Grid are introduced. The drill ends with the Thunderbird School of Business 'Are You Ready' online assessment.

THE OLI FRAMEWORK (creating advantage)

The Future Theme

16. Strategy

This drill introduces a framework for selecting one of four optimal strategic styles (classical, adaptive, shaping, and visionary). The drill ends with an organizational DNA assessment exercise and two interactive online cases (airline operations and pharma pricing).

17. Career

Making the correct career choice is challenging, and very individual. Therefore, this Mini MBA drill introduces career enhancement tools to help everyone succeed (despite the career choice made). The drill ends with an online assessment of how influential a person is in their current workplace and how to increase that influence.

18. Start-up

Harvard Business School research has found that; entrepreneurs will earn 35% less in personal income over a 10-year period, compared to what they could have earned in a paid job. Furthermore, 34% of small businesses fail in the first two years, and 50% fail in the first five years. Therefore, failure is much more common that success in startups. The drill explores the 10 most common causes of startup failure and how to minimize the chances of failure. This drill ends with an online assessment to determine if a person has the characteristics required to succeed as an entrepreneur.

DRILL 1: The Success Formula

'When your mind is telling you that you're done.... you're really only 40 percent done' ~ Navy SEAL

Before reading further, stop for a moment and think about the word SUCCESS. What comes to your mind?

Three questions might have come to your mind;
- What is it?
- How much do I want?
- What must I do to achieve it?

These are important questions which everyone should ask themselves often! But remember; success is a very individual concept. It's individual because there's no one definition, or one magic bullet for achieving it! However, there is research on success which can help to increase the likelihood of achieving success.

External Achievement

Two broad dimensions for defining success were presented in the introduction (external achievement and internal happiness). One common measure for external achievement is money. If you are hoping to achieve success based on that one dimension, consider practicing the '6 Rules for Making Lots of Money'. Those rules are based on the experiences of David Rubenstein, CEO and Co-founder of Carlyle Group. The Carlyle Group have a market cap (total market value), of some $5 billion.

Rubenstein on Making Money

1. **Determination**: Determination is more important that brilliance or intelligence. Characteristics of determination include; not taking no for an answer. According to David, determination can yield far greater financial rewards than will accepting conventional wisdom. However, the secret to being determined is; not to give up on your own beliefs easily or quickly.

2. **Hard Work**: Hard work yields far greater financial rewards than a 9 to 5 work ethic. To realize anything worth achieving in business takes serious time and commitment. If anyone wants to get ahead financially, then long hours are important and a prerequisite.

3. **Focus**: Focus-in on just one subject area where you can truly make yourself an expert. By doing just that, you will become one of your organizations indispensable resources. Therefore, avoid spreading yourself thin early in your career (trying to do and learn too many things), before you learn to do one thing well.

4. **Persuasion**: Learn how to persuade others to do what you want. To be great at persuasion, you must learn how to communicate effectively (writing and speaking).

5. **Be the Best**: Put all your energy into providing the best service/product possible. Therefore, do not focus too much on how much money you wish to make. An obsession with achieving excellence and doing the best job possible (which nobody can do as well as you), is what leads to the making of fortunes. Money must be the happy byproduct, not the principle goal.

6. **Humility**: Humility will lead to far greater success. One should also recognize that 'luck' is likely to play a large role in your success and that bad 'luck' could come along at any moment. Stay humble!

Rubenstein on Failure

"Failure should be viewed as a tool, not as an outcome. If your first get-rich project fails, take what you learned and try something else. Nietzsche said, 'what doesn't kill us makes us stronger'. However, you must avoid the loser's philosophy which states; 'failure makes you stronger and better able to survive future challenges'.

To win, you want to follow the winners' philosophy which says; 'as a result of your failure, you become smarter, more talented, better networked, healthier and more energized. Failure should be viewed as a resource that can be managed." ~ David Rubenstein

Internal Happiness

The Harvard Grant Study has tracked the happiness and health of 268 individual men for over 70 years. George Vaillant (head of research at the study) concludes from the findings so far from the research that: 'the only things that really matter and bring happiness to your life are your relationships with other people'.

The second broad dimension for measuring success is internal happiness. There are three forms of internal happiness (momentary, lifestyle and life-purpose). Professor Richard Shell (Wharton School, University of Pennsylvania), who has been teaching success courses for executive and MBA's for decades has created a Career Success Framework, which incorporates the dimensions of internal happiness.

Career Success Framework

Define Success 'For You'
Have the courage to follow your heart
& intuition (the secret lies within)

Score Card 2
Outer Perspective
- Achievement
- Recognition
- Respect

Trial & Error
Contemplate, take
risks & experiment
- What excites you?

Score Card 1
Inner Feelings
- Fulfillment
- Satisfaction
- Happiness

Focus/Best
What are you better
at than others?

Career Success

Source: Richard Shell

Meaningful work is; work that uses our talents, 'ignites us emotionally,' is financially rewarding, and helps build healthy and strong relationships. One reason so many people are unhappy and disengaged in their jobs today is because they have taken on work that fails to match their skills, interests, and passions (meaningful work).

According to Prof. Shell, those are the true measures of success. Consequently, when considering career planning we must first ask ourselves: what makes my heart sing and what is success for me? This first step includes developing a personal definition of success, or the ideal life we wish to lead, beyond family, friends, and fortune.

The term 'looking-glass self' is used in psychology to explain the insights one can gain from seeing oneself reflected in the looking glass of other people's perceptions (specialist, generalist etc.). Those insights can reveal interest, motivation and much more. This is a useful concept because it is important to remember that everyone's motivation is different (even when they are pursuing the same career). Therefore, trial-and-error may be necessary to identify what really 'ignites us emotionally.' Once we have defined our motivation and 'what we can do better than most others', we can move on to focusing on a specific goal.

Prof. Shell's says that, 78% of 'highly accomplished professionals' cited focused goals as critical to their success. The 'Zeigarnik Effect' explains the power of focus; 'mental crowding in one's consciousness because of unmet goals'. Self-confidence also plays a crucial role on the path to success (faith and confidence).

Finally, a scorecard for one's success should be created and monitored frequently. Prof. Shell reminds us that 'although earning a lot of money can be very good for your sense of pride and self-esteem, money has very little effect on the day-to-day joy you experience, and none whatsoever on the larger, more spiritual dimensions of happiness that many consider the most important in their lives.'

We should also frequently ask ourselves one more important question: 'Imagine we've won the lottery, and money no longer is a primary motivator. Our family is now taken care of, and we've earned a certain amount of notoriety by having the winning ticket. What would we do next in your life? The answer to this one question provides direct access into people's hearts. If we want to be of service to something, that tells us the kind of work we find very meaningful. If we want to teach, this tells us what we find fulfilling right now.'

The Success Formula

Success research has revealed the essential ingredient which must be present to increase our chances of becoming successful! Based on this success research, there is a formula we will now concentrate on. That formula is;

$$2 \times G + TS = Success$$

The success formula was discovered by Prof. Angela Duckworth (University of Pennsylvania). Prof. Duckworth has spent most of her career studying success. Angela has found that success is more likely to be realized if an individual has a high level of 'GRIT'. GRIT is the G in the above formula. The ST represents Skill and Talent (ST).

Predicting Success

Prof. Duckworth carried out GRIT studies on thousands of individuals from varying backgrounds (athletes, business people, artists etc.). One of her studies which is most relevant for this Mini MBA was completed at The United States Military Academy (West Point). West Point is a four-year war college. 1,300 cadets enter West Point every year, and only 70%+- successfully graduate after four years. 55% of a cadet's performance at West Point is based on academic achievement, and 30% on leadership capability.

Prof. Duckworth developed the GRIT Scale Quiz and tested it on West Point Cadets (Plebes). The Plebes were assessed when they first entered the academy, and then at the end of their four years of studies. This was done to try and predict which Plebes were most likely to successfully complete the program.

The GRIT Scale Quiz has been given to more than twelve hundred West Point Plebes, as they embarked on the grueling Bootcamp training (Plebes call this Beast Barracks). The GRIT scores were compared with successful graduations, and the results demonstrated that successful Plebes had much higher than average levels of GRIT. The GRIT Scale Quiz results were found to be a better predictor of success than talent, or intelligence quotient (IQ).

The Success Formula

Prof., Duckworth defines GRIT as; hard work, motivation, and perseverance. For the successful West Point graduates, the levels of GRIT mattered more than leadership qualities, intelligence and even physical fitness. The Duckworth GRIT formula is calculated based on the following components:

$$Talent \times Effort = Skill$$

$$Skill \times Effort = SUCCESS\ (Achievement)$$

Effort is counted twice in the formula, and effort represents GRIT. In other words, Grit has a 2 times impact on success, when compared with skill or talent. Based on the above components, the success formula is calculated as;

2 x G + TS = SUCCESS

What Prof. Duckworth's research findings are telling us is that, nobody gets to be great at something without effort, no matter how good their aptitude (talent and skill). GRIT is the effort part of the equation. Therefore, 'whatever your level of talent, you're still going to have to invest effort to develop that talent and skill... to succeed'. GRIT represents the power of passion and perseverance.

The happy news from this GRIT research is that all of us can learn to be 'Grittier'. However, the challenge is to determine what we need to learn to become 'Grittier'?

Successful People

GRIT can be better understood when we observe the behavior of successful people. Highly successful people, according to Prof.

Duckworth's research, spend countless hours on details, which are frequently neglected, or not noticed at all by others. Those details in fact, are often crucial to their success and never become irrelevant for them. Furthermore, successful people (and real experts), never get bored with details because they are always discovering interesting aspects in those details. By doing so, they become increasingly immersed, even when there are endless details.

However, we should all remember that high levels of GRIT are not the only factor influencing success. Prof. Duckworth says there is a danger if one views GRIT as the single solution to every challenge, because it is not. For example, being in the right place at the right time (planned luck) can also be critical for success to happen. Furthermore, having a life which provides opportunities to excel can also make the difference. In other words, the right conditions (environment) must be present for success to occur. Finally, please remember that GRIT is no substitute for personal character.

TASK: Measuring GRIT

It's now time to measure your level of GRIT! As a matter of fact, you can now complete the same assessment which the West Point 'Plebes' have taken (along with thousands business people). The link below will take you to Prof. Duckworth's GRIT Scale Quiz page. In a matter of just minutes you will get a personal GRIT Score.

Before doing the Grit Scale Quiz, you may be interested to know the average score on that assessment. The average score is 3.6. However, please remember when comparing your GRIT score with the average, that other success factors do come into play. For example, personal levels of self-restraint (delayed gratification) are important in reinforcing GRIT, and levels of self-control also play an important role.

Take the GRIT Scale Quiz now!

LINK: Angela Duckworth GRIT-Scale Quiz
https://goo.gl/Tmx6U7
Note: No registration is required to take the GRIT Scale Quiz

Increasing GRIT

Now that you have completed the GRIT assessment, and you have determined your personal GRIT Score, you might be interested to know how to increase that GRIT Score. To increase GRIT, Prof. Dr. Duckworth recommends four steps.

1. Identify and concentrate on one personal 'burning interest'. This is necessary because, if you are not passionate about something, you'll most likely have less GRIT (this is especially important when considering career choices).
2. Practice that burning interest a lot! This is necessary because practice makes perfect and perfect practice makes success.
3. Link your burning passion with a 'higher purpose'. In other words, how does the passion you are pursuing improve the world at large, or other people?
4. Make every effort to overcome pessimism or negative thinking by developing a 'growth mind-set'. A 'growth mind-set' simply means that you are continually developing yourself, like you are doing right now by completing this Mini MBA Bootcamp! You must practice GRIT long enough for the benefits to become evident.

The most important thing to remember is that, effort counts twice when it comes to success and that GRIT is the effort part of the success equation. GRIT has been proven to predict success more reliably than talent or I.Q. Therefore, no matter what your talent or skill level might be, you must still invest effort to increase your odds of success. High levels of GRIT can also have other benefits which are worth thinking about;

- Increased confidence.
- A more positive attitude.
- Better self-restraint and self-control.
- Improved performance.

DRILL 1: Summary

The happy news for us all is that anyone can become GRITTIER. However, remember that the values within an individual's society do matter (attitudes towards success or winning). In addition, the presence of systemic barriers to success can prevent success from occurring (organizational values and processes).

1. There is a success formula (2 x G + ST = SUCCESS).
   a. G = GRIT, S = Skill and T = Talent.
2. Other factors come into play which can reinforce the positive effects of GRIT (self-restraint and self-control etc.).
3. Anyone can become GRITTIER!

SOURCES:

Denby, D. (2016). The Limits of GRIT. The New Yorker

Shulevitz, J. (2016). Grit, by Angela Duckworth. The New York Times

Duckworth, A. (2016). Grit: Why Talent Needs Drive to Succeed. Wharton, University of Pennsylvania

Shell, R. (2013). Springboard: Launching Your Personal Search for Success. Penguin/Portfolio

Vaillant, G. (2012). Triumphs of Experience: The Men of the Harvard Grant Study. George E. Vaillant

DRILL 2: Success Formula

'A smooth sea never made a skillful sailor' ~ Navy SEAL

Change is Everywhere

Some 70% of all organizational change efforts fail! What might be the reasons for that failure? The ancient Greek philosopher Heraclitus said, 'there is nothing permanent except change'. In today's uncertain and rapidly changing environment, change is constant. We should all remember that rapid change results in high levels of uncertainty, and this makes a manager's job more complex. To better appreciate the role of change in business, it's first important to understand how good we are personally with change. Now ask yourself; how good am I at dealing with change?

- Are you doing everything you can to prevent change from happening?
- Are you a champion for change?

If I had been asked that question 10 or 20 years ago, my answer would have been based on the conditions of the time. That was a time when there was more certainty, stability and things were more predictable. Furthermore, change at that time had a clearly defined start and end, and it often impacted only a few people within an organization. Change today is very different from what it looked like 10 or 20 years ago. Today, there is no end to change and this constant change affects everyone. What this means is that we must all become better at managing change.

Research on Change

We can all learn a great deal from the research on change. Prof. John Kotter (Harvard Business School) has spent the past forty years observing and researching change efforts in thousands of different organizational settings. What Prof. Kotter has learned about change into three categories.

- **Category 1: The Purposes of Change**
  - To increase revenues and profits (decrease costs).
  - To become more effective (more efficient).
  - Both above.

- **Category 2: The Reasons for Change**
  - Falling behind the competition.
  - Not prepared to compete in the future.
  - Too slow in executing tactics (on the market).
  - Too quick to execute tactics but slow in thinking, strategizing and planning those tactics.
  - Too slow to innovate.
  - Too slow or ineffective; for example, when integrating M&As (M&A's refers to mergers and integrations between firms).
  - Too many organizational siloes (prevent effective internal collaboration and communication between departments or units).

- **Category 3: The Accelerators of Change**
  - Tools to make change successful.

The eight Kotter Change Accelerators (stages) can help prevent change management failure from happening in the first place.

The Eight Change Accelerators

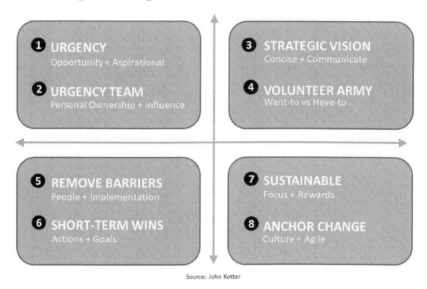

Source: John Kotter

The 8 Accelerators

1. Create a Sense of Urgency

This is the most important accelerator. Therefore, it is critical above everything else to begin by creating a sense of urgency. This urgency must be reinforced throughout any change effort. Failure to implement #1 often results in organizations not having enough of a sense of urgency to drive the necessary change forward. Furthermore, successful change can only begin when there is a minimum of 51% of all employees (75% of management) who believe in that sense of urgency, and who are engaged and energized around the need for change. Creating a sense of urgency sound like an easy thing to achieve, but in fact it's quite a challenge. There are two critical things to keep in mind to successfully create a sense of urgency.

- Urgency must be focused on one single big opportunity. Please pay attention to the word opportunity. The word opportunity is used because; successful change should not and cannot be based on fear (punishment for failure). Fear in fact has not been proven to help accelerate the change process, because only a single big opportunity does.
- Urgency must be positively defined, articulated (clear and understandable), highly energizing, and represent an aspirational description of the future of the organization (what do we all want our organization to be in the future?). Furthermore, it's critical that people must wish to contribute towards achieving that opportunity, and not dread the fear of what might happen if they don't. This is because a good sense of urgency motivates people to buy into the necessary change. However, it is also essential that everyone must also understand why they need to act now.

Urgency highlights the goals of any change plan and more importantly, that urgency shows how those goals will benefit the whole organization. In fact, Prof. Kotter says that creating a sense of urgency is the fuel for all the other change accelerators.

2. Form an Urgency Team

Before any change can occur, one needs to build a guiding team (coalition). Furthermore, that team is made up of a group of people who buy into the planned change, in a strong way (take personal ownership). The team must also involve key people in the organization (not only top management). This is important because, urgency team members will become the 'Ambassadors' of change throughout the organization. In very larger organizations, urgency teams might consist of 35-40 people, who are then further divided into smaller groups.

The urgency team should set a collegial (united) and collaborative tone, which becomes 'infectious'. The urgency team must also embody the principle of; 'what they do, speaks so loudly, that others can hear what they say.' Senior executives of an organization must be a part of the discussion on change, but they don't drive the process. This is because;

peer-to-peer influence (employee-to-employee, manager-to-manager) is much more powerful than executive influence.

How to Identify Urgency Team Members

- Recruit people who have demonstrated peer-to-peer influence over time in the organization.
- Recruit people who are highly regarded and respected by their colleagues and peers.
- Recruit people who have a lot of tenacity (GRIT) and who are recognized by others.
- Recruit people who don't care about who get the credit, (as opposed to those people who are ego-driven).
- Recruit people who have an 'abundance mentality' (they view change as an opportunity to get together and do-it). Abundance mentality is the very opposite to 'I'm doing this for my own visibility or personal benefit'.

Clearly and precisely defining the urgency team membership criteria helps in recruiting the best people. This is important because those people will drive the urgency and by doing so, help the organization achieve successful change.

3. Formulate A Strategic Vision

According to Prof. Kotter, the mistake many leaders make during most change programs is that they start the change processes from the strategic vision stage (#3). Try to avoid this mistake and remember that strategic vision must always follow establishing a sense of urgency and creating the urgency team.

Strategic vision means that the organization develops a strategy, and that strategy is communicated aggressively to the larger group. The strategy needs to be defined in detail, must be crystal clear and concise. A critical part of the strategic vision is that one must also define and create the specific initiatives (actions) which are necessary to reach small milestones, throughout the whole change process. Those small milestones are the points when some defined progress is made, or some of the necessary activities are completed. Milestones, when achieved one small step at a time, help direct the organization towards its end goal. Furthermore, everyone likes to make progress.

4. Recruit Volunteer Army

John Heywood (English poet c. 1497. c. 1580) once said 'many hands make light work'. Therefore, to achieve successful change, one must also enlist a volunteer army (many hands). This is important because, many hands will lighten the work. The urgency team must communicate the change-strategy, vision and initiatives, to the volunteer army. Their goal is to gain buy-in or personal ownership to the idea of change from the army. One critical principle for achieving buy-in is that people should volunteer to be part of the effort, and not be demanded to do so. This is important because, the volunteer army puts change into action and drives many of the short-term wins and early change efforts.

Volunteers must also have a want-to versus have-to attitude. Please remember that having a want-to attitude is critical for all eight accelerators. When people are excited about pursuing change, above and beyond a day job, the company is on the way towards successful change. This is because the volunteer army wants to! However, the challenge is; how do to instill the feeling of want-to in people?

To instill a want-to attitude requires sustainable, infectious, and viral change, as opposed to using a change toolkit that just grinds through some generic process (one size fits all). Volunteers must also be kept informed about what's most critical (this is done through a few key people across the business). Furthermore, one must discover issue about which the volunteer army is excited. However, those issues must be based on the organization's strategic priorities. In addition, volunteers must be allowed to volunteer or self-organize around ideas for which they have the most passion. Finally, the direction must be defined and team leaders allowed to support that direction.

5. Remove Barriers

It's easy to lose momentum (energy) when obstacles are encountered during the process of change. Therefore, any obstacles that may prevent progress need to be removed immediately. People can and often do prevent change from happening but remember that the support of 51% of the people in an organization is enough to be successful in a change effort (75% of management). Despite this support, the other 49% of people may be skeptical (suspicious), or even cynical (make fun of) of the proposed change. Therefore, the important message which the guiding coalition should give to those skeptical people is that; 'we ask that you don't actively block us trying to make a difference but there is no need for you to join us right now.'

6. Achieve Short-Term Wins

It is vital during any change process to generate short-term wins' all along the way. This is because; progress and frequent small successes motivate the volunteer army and the guiding coalition. Furthermore, the successful completion of smaller initiatives (actions), when combined, will be essential in successfully reaching the end-goal. Please remember though; it is vital to define, achieve and communicate frequently those short-term wins.

7. Sustain Acceleration

It is one thing to achieve short term wins, but the real goal is continuous and sustained progress towards the longer-term goals of the organization. Therefore, throughout the process everyone must stay focused on repeated wins.

8. Anchor CHANGE

Anchoring change means that 'change becomes part of the organization's culture.' Therefore, continuous efforts must be made to ensure that change is accepted and viewed as an opportunity throughout the organization, even in the future. This is because having a positive view of change will make any future strategic initiatives (actions) easier to achieve, and by doing so will help to create a more agile organization.

Implementation Principles

All this talk about change is exciting however, talk and even effort is often not enough. This is because; the critical element for successful change to happen is implementation. Therefore, Prof. Kotter (Harvard) recommends four ways to help assure the successful implementation of any change effort. Those four principles are very simple, so beware (within simplicity - is often hidden - complexity)!

1. Management vs. Leadership

Transformational change (a life-changing event) requires more leadership (doing the right things), than management (doing things right). However, more does not only mean more leaders! What more really means is that, organizations need to create more moments where 'all employees' can demonstrate leadership.

2. Head vs. Heart

Transformational change 'must be driven by people's hearts, passions, emotions, and aspirations to do something extraordinary, as opposed to fear'. Prof. Kotter refers to heads and hearts because the head still matters (logic and rigor still count).

3. Want-to vs Have-to

What this means in simple terms is that 51% of all the people in the organization must want to change (75% of management).

4. Few vs Many

This principle recognizes the necessary shift from a 'few experts' leading a change to 'activating many' throughout the organization. These four principles can support the execution of Kotter's eight change accelerators, and they will make the greatest difference possible.

DRILL 2: Summary

1. A strategy for change should only be developed after urgency is established and forming the guiding coalition (urgency team).
2. Volunteers are more powerful than people who are only acting out of fear; 'many hands make light work.'
3. Change must be driven by peoples' hearts, passions, emotions, and aspirations to do something extraordinary. The role of managers (leaders) is to release that passion in others.

TASK: Change Skills Assessment

Take the change skills assessment now! This MindTools quiz assesses where people are strong, and where they need to develop new change management skills.

LINK: How Good Are Your Change Management Skills?
https://goo.gl/ZwxJBv
Note: No registration is required to take the quiz

SOURCES:

Kotter, J. (2007). Leading Change. Why Transformation Efforts Fail. Harvard Business Review

Rao, H. (2015). How to Lead Change Within Your Organization. Stanford Graduate School of Business

Meaney, M. (2014). McKinsey on Change Management. McKinsey & Co.

DRILL 3: Success Formula

'It pays to be a winner' ~ Navy SEAL

Google search the term organizational theory and there will be some 15 million hits. Nobody has the time to read 15 million hits. Another alternative is to look at Wikipedia. Wikipedia defines organizational theory as follows;

'Organization theory is characterized by vogues, heterogeneity, claims and counterclaims', and even greater differentiation in theory and practice has developed. Developments in the theory and prescriptions for practice show disagreement about the purposes and uses of a theory of organization, the issues to which it should address itself (such as supervisory style and organizational culture), and the concepts and variables that should enter into such a theory.' Google Search

That Wikipedia definition is a mouth full, and really does not help very much. Therefore, in this Mini MBA drill we won't get into the 'vogues, heterogeneity, claims or counterclaims' referred to by Wikipedia, and we won't look at 15 million Google hits. Rather, we will focus-in on the most relevant question about organizations that should be of value to any manager, and that question is;

'How can a manager design and support effective and efficient structures and processes in their organization, to achieve the desired results?'

Please pay attention to 'in their organization', because every organization is unique in one way or another. Therefore, any organization action taken must reflect this uniqueness.

Complexity

When discussing organizations in this Mini MBA Bootcamp, we are going to follow the 'KISS' principle (keep it simple stupid). Therefore, to keep it simple, imagine for a moment that it's Monday morning in the office, and a manager is having their Monday pow-wow (meeting) with members of their management team. During team meetings, any manager who is concerned about the organization might ask some of the following organization KISS questions;

1. What is driving our business performance at the front- line (the front-line of most organizations represents 50-60% of a company's management activity and up to 80% of the workforce who are directly facing customers)?
2. Are our costs rising too fast, no matter what we have been trying to do to prevent that from happening?
3. Who in the team is responsible for that front-line performance?
4. How long does it take us to make decisions?

Why should a manager ask the four questions just listed? Well, they should ask these questions because, complex structures and processes creep into every business, and by doing so they lower the levels of performance (effectiveness and efficiency). The KISS questions are one way of uncovering that complexity.

Detecting complexity is important because complexity has a direct impact on performance, and performance is one of the primary responsibilities of managers in every organization. However, one should not forget that there is good complexity and bad complexity. Good complexity can be healthy when it is used to one's advantage, Bad complexity, on the other hand, results in lower performance. However, the challenge for every manager is to avoid or remove bad complexity, while simultaneously designing-in good complexity. To better understand complexity, there are three important questions to ask;

- What is it?
- How does it occur?
- How to minimize, if not remove it, entirely?

What is Complexity?

Please remember that simple, complicated and complex are not the same thing. Simple systems involve some basic issues, which over time can be mastered (following a food recipe for example). Complicated systems, on the other hand have many moving parts, although those parts do have a common pattern of movement (rocket engine design for example). Once one is familiar with a complicated problem (system), it's possible to solve that problem also in the future.

Complex systems on the other hand often behave in ways that are constantly changing, self-organizing, and evolving (raising children is a good example). Because of this constant change and evolution, complex systems are often unpredictable and cannot be understood by using simple or complicated approaches for solving problems (evidence, policy, planning and management etc.). When managers are dealing with complex organizational challenges they must also understand the different form of complexity.

4 Forms of Complexity

- **Imposed Complexity:** Includes laws, and regulations which are imposed, and not easily managed.
- **Inherent Complexity:** Involves things which are often inherited with a business (the givens). Often the only way to remove these is by stopping the activity.
- **Designed Complexity:** Results from choices about where the business operates (what it sells, to whom, and how). This form of complexity can be removed, but unnecessarily changing a business model can have negative implications on a business.
- **Unnecessary Complexity:** Influence the essential alignment between organizational needs and processes supporting those needs. Unnecessary complexity is manageable however, it first needs to be identified.

Four Forms of Complexity

Source: McKinsey & Company

How Complexity Occurs

Chris Zook and James Allen (Bain and Co.) have carried out research on complexity in 8,000 global companies. Their research findings show that every business, almost always, becomes too complex (bureaucracy creeps in). When this happens, it can slow down everything, especially decision making. Some of the most common symptoms of bad complexity in an organization can be detected when one begins to hear people making some of the following statements;

- ▪ 'We're losing touch with customers' (we no longer understand them).
- ▪ 'We're drowning in processes and PowerPoints' (those processes have become more important than the reason we are doing them in the first place).
- ▪ 'We're no longer able to act decisively or precisely'.

Two-thirds of the companies researched by Zook and Allen faced serious complexity challenges at one time or another over the 15 years of their research. Fifty of the largest companies studied faced prolonged complexity challenges, which had a serious impact on their performance. Therefore, to better understand complexity it should be investigated from two different levels (business level complexity and process level complexity). At the business level, complexity can occur because of;

- Lack of understanding by management of what drives value in the business.
- Lack of the necessary linkages between; customers, costs, and capability sharing within the organization.
- Lack of strategic focus or clarity (alignment with growth).
- Lack of performance metrics (management information systems).
- Too many organizational layers (levels-siloes).

Complexity can also occur at the process level of an organization. This can be seen when there are too many non-critical processes (preventing people from focusing on critical things). Furthermore, the organizational capability might not be fit-for-purpose (potential is lacking, or it is in the wrong places). Finally, accountability is separated from actions and responsibility is separated from actions. What this means is that; process complexity has separated accountability from actions, and responsibility from those actions (they are not linked).

How to Minimize Complexity

The first step in minimizing complexity is to; understand the complexity. A common mistake made by managers when they recognize complexity is to 'avoid it or try to quickly fix the symptoms', before they investigate the more complete picture. However, this can be a waste of time, especially when the problem is systemic (for example the organizations operating model is broken). Therefore, managers must begin with a diagnosis of the complexity (is the complexity; imposed, inherent, designed, or unnecessary?).

1. Identify Complexity Origin

The next step is to identify the origin of the complexity. However, the real causes of complexity are often difficult to identify because they are hidden in multiples places. Therefore, managers should explore the origins of complexity across the organization and, especially at the interfaces (between different business units and functions).

2. Activity Reduction

Complexity reduction is in fact all about activity reduction therefore, to reduce complexity; managers must eliminate activities that do not generate value, along with identifying duplication of activities. However, it is necessary to be cautious at this stage because managers must always consider the impact on efficiency of any actions they might take. In addition, it is essential to keep in mind the needs of the front-line. Furthermore, managers should always follow the complexity-reduction philosophy of;

- Do less.
- Do it better.
- Do it only once.
- Do it in the right places.

3. Driven from the Top

The leadership team must also be fully committed to reducing complexity. If they are not, the imposed changes will never work. More importantly, this also means that leadership must change their behavior first, because if that does not happen, nothing will happen. Nothing happens because employees always know when their behavior is expected to change, but not the behavior of the leaders. Therefore, it is essential that leaders first; make sure that they have;

- Identified and documented the root-causes of the complexity.
- Defined a few actions to address complexity exactly and continually.

- Defined the rewards for actions taken to reduce-eliminate complexity (for example a better working environment for all or better results).

4. Implementation

Implementation is often the weakest phase in any complexity reduction program. This means that even though managers might have identified the unnecessary complexity and its causes, the solutions for removing that complexity still fail. They fail because management did not agree with front-line personnel on what needs to be done.

5. Identify Risks

All the risks must be identified. However, avoiding those identified risks can only be achieved by defining specific actions for each risk.

6. Culture

Finally, changing the behaviors and mindsets of people is one of the biggest challenges in any complexity reduction program. When thinking about changing behavior and mindsets, reflect on the first three steps in every change process which covered in an earlier Bootcamp drill;

- Create a Sense of Urgency.
- Form a Team.
- Develop a Strategy.

Often, managers try to change too many behaviors all at once and forget to explain what the complexity reduction changes mean for every person and every process. Applying the KISS rule can be helpful at this final stage;

- Define just two or three critical desired behaviors' which will make the process a success.
- Define two to three practical implications for management and the front-line.
- Define two to three daily behaviors and activities that will support the process (for example feedback and coaching others).

- Demonstrate commitment to the process every day and continually reinforce the principle that; meeting the promises made is essential to make the desired behaviors permanent.

DRILL 3: Summary

1. There are four forms of complexity; imposed, inherent, designed and unnecessary.
2. Complexity should be investigated at the business level and process level
3. Change must be driven by peoples' hearts, passions, emotions, and aspirations to do something extraordinary. The role of managers (leaders) is to release that passion in others.

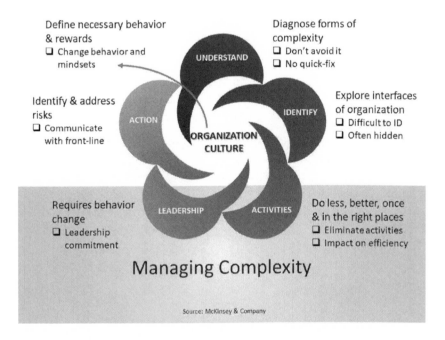

Managing Complexity

Source: McKinsey & Company

TASK: Complexity Assessment

A manager's behavior and attitude influence organizational complexity. Therefore, the first step to reducing complexity, starts at an individual level. Take the FutureThink complexity assessment below to evaluate how your behavior and attitude to complexity might influence your management effectiveness.

LINK: FutureThink Complexity Quiz
https://goo.gl/QcVrdr
Note: No registration is required to take the quiz

SOURCES:

Lichtenau, T., Smith, J., & Sophie Horrocks (2015). Tackling Complexity: How to Create Simple and Effective Organizations. Bain & Company

Wade, M. (2016). The Legacy of Success. IMD

Zook, C., & Allen, J. (2016). The Founders Mentality. Bain and Company

DRILL 4: Innovation

'Nothing lasts forever' ~ Navy SEAL

In this Mini MBA drill, we will focus on two critical innovation questions;

1. How does a company become great at innovation?
2. Who are the most innovative companies in world today (what we can learn from them)?

According to the Boston Consulting Group (BCG), innovation is one of the top three priorities for 80% of companies today. BCG have carried out one of the longest running and respected rankings of the most innovative companies in the world (since 2005). During every year of those studies, innovation was ranked by the 1500 senior executives who participated as one of their top 3 strategic priorities. What this tells us is that innovation is worthy of considering during this Mini MBA Bootcamp.

Three Forms of Innovation

Innovation can mean many different things. However, every manager must understand that innovation is not the same as invention. Google the word invention and one gets the following definition;

The action of inventing something new, typically a process or device or a creative ability'.

Pay attention to the Google definition of invention; **something new was created**. However, does this mean the invention was of use to anybody? It Does not!

1. Disruptive Innovation

The 1st form of innovation is called Disruptive Innovation. Disruptive innovations often contain common off-the-shelf components that are easily available, but they are put together in a new way (simpler than existing approaches). In other words, disruptive innovations are used for solving the same kind of problems as existing approaches. However, disruptive innovations provide a more attractive solution to existing problems.

Disruptive innovations often have fewer features (attributes). One very important point to remember is that disruptive innovations frequently do not provide what customers in established markets might want. What this means is that disruptive innovations are not usually targeted at established markets in the beginning. Rather, they are targeted to emerging market segments. In practice this means that; disruptive innovations are targeted at markets or customers who are more remote from, and unimportant to the mainstream existing markets of companies.

Therefore, established companies often ignore those disruptions because 'potential customers' are not considered attractive. Please remember this important point, because it is one of the main reasons that disruptive innovation occurs in the first place. Disruptive innovations make products or services more affordable and accessible to a larger base of customers who were not served earlier. Furthermore, one of the great things about disruptive innovations is that they create growth and jobs. However, disruptive innovations need a lot of financial capital (money) to be developed successfully. They need that money because, disruptive innovations consume a lot of cash during the concept development phase; testing, marketing, and getting customers to accept new ways of doing things.

2. Sustaining Innovation

The 2nd form of innovation according to Prof. Christensen is called sustaining innovation. Sustaining innovations do not create new markets but they help in developing existing markets. They do this by providing better value to those existing markets. Sustaining innovations provide better value because they encourage existing companies on a market to compete against each other's sustaining improvements. Therefore, sustaining innovations are focused primarily on making existing good products even better. However, sustaining innovations also have a positive impact on a company's profit margin, and market share. Unfortunately, sustaining innovations do not often create net growth on a market, because they simply improve existing solutions for existing customers.

3. Efficiency Innovation

The 3rd form of innovation is called efficiency innovations. Efficiency innovations reduce the cost of making and distributing existing products and services. However, efficiency innovations almost always reduce the number of jobs in an industry. They do so because efficiency innovations allow the same amount of work (or more) to get done, but they use fewer people or resources to achieve this increased output. One might be thinking that efficiency innovations are not good for a market or an economy. However, although efficiency innovations do eliminate jobs, they also increase a company's free cash flow, which is a very good thing. Increasing free cash flow is a good thing because it means that the free cash flow made available can (and should) flow back into the development of new disruptive innovations (at least in theory). Free cash flow might be a new term for some, but rather than discussing this in detail now, we will discuss free cash flow in the Finance and Accounting Drills.

These three forms on innovation should work together in what Prof. Christensen calls the 'economic engine'. The way the economic engine should work is that; disruptive innovations create jobs and sustaining/efficiency innovations create cash. In theory, the cash created is moved back into developing more disruptive innovations, and the cycle repeats itself. This cycle is essential because disruptive innovations need a lot of cash (capital), for them to be developed successfully on a market.

Innovation Drivers

Now that we all know more about the different forms of innovation, let's return to the two questions we asked at the beginning of this drill. The first of those questions was;

How does a company become great at innovation?

According to the BCG research, there are three primary reasons (drivers) that the world's most innovative companies are great innovators. Those reasons are; speed, processes, and technology platforms.

Speed

Speed means that the best innovators in the world are very fast. They are faster in development new products, new technologies and new solutions which the market needs. Speed means that great innovators have a better return on innovation investment (RII). However, more importantly than just being fast, great innovators also know how to identify and set the right priorities. What this means is that great innovators can identify and prioritize the adoption of the best new technologies available. It's important to remember this point and to remember that in today's fast paced world, speed can be a major advantage for any company.

Processes

The second reason great innovators are great is because of their processes. They are great at adopting and deploying lean processes. Lean process might be a new term for some however; lean processes are becoming increasingly important for every business. By lean processes, we mean that great innovators are continuously focusing on creating more value for customers, but with fewer resource inputs. This means that great innovators are very strong at incremental (small steps) improvements. They are great at this because they are following the lean philosophy of; build, test, learn and rebuild (BTLR).

The BTLR cycle (with emphasis on the word cycle), has in fact become an essential process for all great innovators. As a matter of fact, the best innovators (according to BCG) are 2x or 3x times more likely to have already adopted lean processes.

Everyone is now more curious about 'lean thinking' or they are already hearing a lot about it in their company. We will discuss lean more deeply in the Operations Drill. For now, though, it is enough to remember that;

- Lean processes create more value, but with fewer resources.
- Lean processes focus on continuous incremental (small step) improvements.
- Lean companies practice the philosophy of; Build, Test, Learn and Rebuild (in a continuous cycle).

Technology Platforms

The third source of great innovation (according to BCG) is technology platforms. In simple terms, a technology platform is a group of technologies that are used as a base upon which other applications (processes or technologies) can be developed. A good example of the 'platform' principle can be seen in personal computing. The computer platform is in fact the basic hardware (the computer), and software (the operating system), upon which software applications can be run. Technology platforms allow different applications and activities to operate more effectively and improve the connectivity between applications and activities. Therefore, it is no surprise that leading innovators are developing technology platforms all the time. Many of those platform developments involve big data and analytics because this helps great innovators to also make better management decisions.

One of the most important things about platforms to remember is that they should be scalable. Another way to say this is; the platform can be rapidly increased in size, while remaining effective and efficient. Scalability is very important in today's business environment because it allows a system, network, or process to handle a growing amount of work and to be enlarged quickly, to meet growing demand on a market. Don't worry about these 'buzz words' like lean and scalable at this point, because we will get into these more during later drills. For now, it is important to just remember that;

1. Speed is critical to be great at innovation.
2. The right processes result in faster performance (BTLR-B).
3. Platforms help great innovators to scale their business; quickly, effectively and efficiently.

TASK: Innovation Booster Exercise

To better understand organizational innovation, now review the 'Innovation Booster Exercise' checklist below and consider what action might be needed to boost your organizations innovation capability.

Innovation Booster Exercise

QUESTION	ISSUES	REQUIRED ACTIONS
WHO	Should increasing innovation be a priority?	
WHAT	What specific activity or process to focus on?	
WHERE	Where in the process is the innovation bottleneck?	
HOW	Proposed changes and how to implement them?	
WHEN	At what time... sequence etc.?	
WHY	What are the benefits of the actions taken and success measures?	

Innovation @Google

Let's now move on to the 2nd question raised at the start of this drill, and that question was;

Who are the most innovative companies in world today (and why)?

Understanding the most innovative companies is very important to understand because we can learn a great deal from the best.

According to Boston Consulting Group (BCG), research rankings; Apple Corporation is the #1 innovator in the world followed by Google at #2 and Tesla at #3. For the remaining discussion on innovation, we will focus-in on Google. We'll do this because most people are familiar with Google and Google's business activities. Furthermore, most people are probably using one of Google's products regularly (if not multiple times every day). There are many innovative lessons from Google, but for the purposes of this drill it is important to consider; how have Google managed to be the 2nd best innovator in the world for the past nine years in a row (BCG research)?

The answer to that question is not simple. However, one could summarize the reasons by saying that; successful innovation at Google occurs because they have mastered nine different innovation capabilities. By the way, those nine critical innovation capabilities are based on the opinions of real Google manager's. The nine innovation capabilities at Google could be placed into three different innovation buckets;

1. Purpose, Talent and Doing the impossible.
2. Openness, Sharing, and a Data driven mindset.
3. Simple, Fast, and Always being user-focused.

Let's now discuss each of these Google capabilities, one at a time.

Innovation Bucket #1

The most important innovation driver for Google is in Bucket #1; **The Purpose of Google**. Purpose at Google means; 'the work Google does can have and does have, an impact on millions of people in a positive way.' Now that might sound a bit vague or unclear, but Googlers believe it, and they are guided by it every single day.

The purpose of 'can have and do have an impact on millions of people in a positive way' is realized in Google by investing-in, developing, and retaining strong managers. This means that successful Google managers;

- Have a clear team vision and strategy.
- Are great coaches.
- Have a genuine interest & concern for their team.
- Are always focused on productivity & results.
- Are good communicators and listeners?
- Have the essential technical skills.

In addition to purpose and great management, Innovation Bucket #1 at Google also contains a culture of thinking that, 'what is possible, is 10 times more possible than what one could ever imagine'. Or as Google refer to it, the 10x Rule. The 10x Rule states that 'great just isn't good enough'. Please remember that when thinking about your organization!

Innovation Bucket #2

The second innovation bucket at Google is filled with the principle of 'ideas can come from anywhere'. Ideas can come from anywhere sounds simple, but at Google those ideas must also be measured and validated, and that is something many companies forget to address. The most important philosophy behind 'ideas can come from everywhere' is that Googlers believe if you give people freedom, they will amaze you! To illustrate this important Google way of thinking, the 20% Projects yield some of the best ideas. 20% Projects allow employees for one-day-a-week to work on personal-but-relevant side projects. What this means is that 20% of an employee's time at Google can be directed towards personal but relevant side projects which they can personally select.

Innovation Bucket #3

Finally, the 3rd innovation bucket at Google is filled with processes. Bucket #3 allows Google to continuously re-invent existing processes, concepts and products. The goal of this is to spearhead ideas that many can benefit from. At Google this philosophy is often qualified through the Toothbrush Test. In principle, everything Google does should pass the Toothbrush Test (does the product/service solve simple problems that people have on an everyday basis). If you're interested in learning more about the Toothbrush Test at Google, just Google 'Larry page toothbrush test 'and you will find out more about the Google process for qualifying ideas.

Fast is also better than slow at Google. Fast at Google means that they apply the BTLR-B process; Build, Test, Learn, and Re-Build, or what some might call rapid-learning. However, here is an important point to remember about rapid innovation at Google. Google know that speed can sometimes be dangerous, and often results in failure. However, at Google there is no shame or stigma attached to failure. As a matter of fact, the Google mantra is 'If you do not fail often, you are not trying hard enough'. This mantra is very important to remember when thinking about successful innovation in any organization.

Another important point to be aware of is that Google are not focused on the competition. They are in fact focused solely on Google users. This means that the primary goal at Google is to always help users 'amplify moments that matter'. To achieve that goal, Google are continuously trying to show users 'the magic'. Google are doing this because, by showing people 'the magic', they are winning users love and trust. Continuously trying to win customer love and trust helps companies like Google remain innovative.

DRILL 4: SUMMARY

1. There are three forms of innovation:
   a. Disruptive: Make products more affordable and accessible.
   b. Sustaining: Make existing products even better.
   c. Efficiency: Eliminate jobs but increase free cash flow.
2. Three capabilities of great innovators:
   a. Speed: Faster at almost everything.
   b. Lean Thinking: Strong at continuous incremental improvements.
   c. Technology Platforms: Adopting and deploying quickly enabling technologies.
3. Purpose is essential however, creating purpose requires that one to invest in building and retaining strong managers.

TASK: Innovation Attitude

People fall into five broad categories of attitude towards innovation. Take this online assessment and find out which category you may fall into.

LINK: Nesta Innovation Quiz
https://goo.gl/dF9bCe
Note: No registration is required to take the quiz

TASK: Organization Innovation Assessment

Find out in minutes your companies level of innovation management expertise.

LINK: Sopheon Innovation Management Level Quiz
https://goo.gl/gP3Cv4
Note: No registration is required to take the quiz

SOURCES:

Kallayil, G. (2013). Google's 9 Principles of Innovation. San Francisco Dream Summit

Christensen, C. (2016). The Innovator's Dilemma. Startup Grind Global 2016

DRILL 5: Management

'I lead by example in all situations' ~ Navy SEAL

For just one moment, think about this important question;

What should a manager be doing?

What activities should be a top priority for every manager? When asked this question above, one might first have thought about a management situation they are familiar with. Maybe it was a case of excellent management, and what that excellent management looked like. Or maybe one was thinking about a case where management had failed, and why that was the case... what did they do wrong?

'Leadership is about doing the right things, but management is about doing things right.' Peter Drucker said that. Ducker also said that; 'any discussion on management must first begin with the tasks to be performed, and their performance.' This statement is enough to understand the meaning of management. However, in this Mini MBA drill we will consider more deeply Drucker's definition of the primary tasks of a manager. We shall do this to really understand what it means to be a manager.

Drucker divided the job of the manager into five basic tasks:

1. Setting objectives.
2. Organizing.
3. Motivating and communicating.
4. Measuring performance.
5. Developing people.

Five Tasks of a Manager

Let's now go through each of these five tasks of a manager, in order that we can understand them better.

1. Setting Objectives

The 1st task of the manager is setting objectives. According to Drucker, the manager sets goals for a group, and then decides what work needs to be done to meet those goals. However, along with deciding on the necessary goals and work to be done; those goals and the work to be done to achieve them, must enhance the economic performance of the business! This is important to remember because according to Drucker, 'management and only management can justify its existence and authority based solely on the economic results it produces'.

Drucker also said that, 'the management of any business has failed if it fails to produce economic results'. In other words, management has failed if it does not supply goods and services which are desired by consumers at price consumers are willing to pay. Management has also failed if it does not improve, or at least maintain, the wealth-producing capacity of the economic resources entrusted to it. According to Drucker, the real purpose of management is in fact 'the responsibility for profitability'. **This means that the primary task of management is to set objectives and optimize the economic output of the firm**!

What are you're feeling about statement just made? Maybe you're thinking... what about the people, what about the best interest of employees... the customers or society as a whole? Well Drucker does consider those factors in his philosophy of management, but let's come back to those ideas in a moment if that's ok.

If we are to follow the principle meaning of management according to Peter Drucker; managers take the responsibility for profitability by setting the objectives which help the business achieve profitability and optimize economic output! To help managers achieve these objectives Drucker invented the concept of Management by Objectives (MBO). MBO means that; managers measure the performance of employees in comparison to the typical standards for the job they might be completing. However, when practicing MBO managers must remember to follow four important rules;

1. Managers must ensure that the chosen objectives are aligned with the corporate vision and mission (strategy).
2. Managers must define individual goals for each individual objective.
3. Managers must decide what must be done, to reach those objectives.
4. Managers must actively and effectively communicate the objectives to those people whose performance is needed, to achieve those objectives.

S.M.A.R.T. Criteria

Drucker also said that, 'if employees help determine the MBO activities along with the standards of performance, they will be much more likely to fulfill them'. However, to ensure successful fulfillment of those roles, it is important to make sure that the objectives are valid and relevant. To guarantee that validity, those objectives should meet the SMART Criteria;

S   Specific Objectives.
M   Measurable Objectives.
A   Achievable Objectives.
R   Realistic Objectives.
T   Time-bound Objectives (within a specific start and stop time).

2. Organizing

The 2nd task of the manager is organizing. Organizing groups of people involves;

- Analyzing the activities, decisions, and relations needed.
- Classifying the work to be done.
- Dividing the work into manageable activities and manageable jobs.
- Grouping units and jobs into an organization structure.
- Selecting people for the management of the units and jobs to be done.

To effectively divide work and to select the right people, according to Drucker, requires decentralization. In other words, to achieve the desired results it is better to delegate tasks and in doing so give employees more power. Although delegation and giving power to employees is necessary, empowering (or giving that power to employees) can in fact be very difficult to achieve. This is because empowering employees also means;

- Giving them leadership.
- Giving them a clearly defined function to perform.
- Giving them more responsibility and the necessary incentives (or motivators).
- Giving them rewards.
- Giving them status (recognition).

Effectively empowering employees also requires high levels of trust in management, and the belief and trust by managers that every individual employee can perform the required tasks. According to Drucker, there are many benefits in having empowered employees. The most important benefit is the satisfaction those employees will gain through their job and the work they do! This empowerment philosophy may seem obvious at first, but often this simple philosophy is poorly practiced in business today.

3. Motivating & Communicating

The 3rd task of the manager is to motivate and communicate. Drucker called this the 'integrating' function of the manager. Effective integration (motivation and communication) requires managers to do the following;

- Make a team out of people who are responsible for various jobs.
- Tell people what their job involves.
- Support the team in producing economic goods and services, which will have a positive impact on people, communities, and society.

The biggest motivation and communication challenge a manager faces are when trying to balance the tension between the work employees carry out, and the amount of effort they put into that work. Please remember that balancing this tension of work vs. effort is very important for management, because that balance will have an immediate and positive impact on performance. That balancing act is essential because; business performance must come first. Performance must come first because it is 'the primary aim of the enterprise, and the only reason for its existence'. Therefore, it is important that; without good performance, 'companies are unable to contribute to societal and other issues'. In addition to this, managers must always strive to resolve the ever-present work-effort tension. If a manager cannot resolve this tension, at least they should try to make it as productive as possible.

Contributing to societal and other issues is becoming an increasingly important role for managers. Drucker recognized this fact much earlier than most other academics. The reason this is happening is because increasingly society is looking to business for leadership on the quality of people's lives! Therefore, accountability for the social dimensions of business is also part of the manager's task. To manage that task effectively means that managers must also consider the business impact on the community as a neighbor, a source of jobs, tax revenue and how their company contributes as best as possible to the fundamental concern for the quantities of life and the environment. And here is a very important point to remember, 'if the work and the worker are mismanaged in a business, there will be no business performance, and if there is no business performance, the quality of life will suffer'.

4. Measuring Performance

The 4th task of the manager is to measure performance. Measuring performance means that managers must establish the appropriate targets and yardsticks, to analyze, appraise and interpret performance. Every manager must remember that one of their primary tasks is to measure performance in the 'here and now'. To do that well they will need to;

- Create measurements which are focused on the performance of the whole organization and every individual staff member.
- Analyze, appraise and interpret performance based on those measurements.

- Communicate the meaning of those measurements and their findings to subordinates (people who work for them) leaders, and other managers.

When communicating performance, it is very important to have accurate and understandable data to support that communication. One effective way to quantify performance measurement and make it more understandable for everyone, is to use Key Performance Indicators (KPI's). However, to effectively use KPI's, one must first select the best KPI's for their specific business activities. Making that selection requires one to;

- Define the business processes (or BP's) in question.
- Define the requirements for those business processes.
- Establish quantitative and qualitative measurements of the desired results and ways to compare those with goals.
- Decide how to manage the difference between the goals & achieved measures, along with determining how to adjust processes to achieve those desired goals.

Measuring performance and maintaining that performance in the future brings the 'time factor' into the equation. This time factor is always important because management must consider both the present and the future (short-run and long-run). When doing that, it's important to remember that keeping the enterprise or business performing in the present time, means that there will be an enterprise capable of performing in the future. Therefore, making short-term profits at the cost of future financial health, may mean that the survival of that business comes into question. Because of this profit-time dimension, one important role of the manager is to make the company capable of performance, growth, and change in the future. This is essential because if managers cannot do that, they have in fact destroyed the capital of the business. In other words, 'they have destroyed the capacity of resources in the business to produce wealth tomorrow'.

Considering the future raises many challenges because; 'the only thing we know about the future is that it is going to be different'. Therefore, uncertainty must be considered by managers always. The time-dimension which is causing uncertainty, is a unique characteristic of managerial decision making. It is unique because, unlike many other forms of decision making, managerial decision making involves acting based on present conditions and on the unknown future. However, despite all the uncertainty the future might bring, 'by ensuring that the enterprise is strong today means that the enterprise will more likely also succeed in the future'. Therefore, one of the primary tasks of a manager is to measures performance in the 'here and now'.

5. Developing People

The 5th and final task of the manager is to develop people. This means that managers also act as administrators. This task has taken on added importance for managers recently due to the rise of the 'knowledge worker' (workers whose main capital is their knowledge). In a knowledge economy employee are the company's most important assets therefore, it's up to the manager to develop that asset. However, when managing those people, one must also keep in mind performance.

There are many additional challenges which managers face when developing people. For example; who should be developed etc.? When considering how best to develop people the manager should always consider the following optimization decisions;

- Define which of the organizations offerings, activities or people produce extraordinary economic results or can produce those results.
- Determine which of the markets and/or end uses in the market place, can help produce extraordinary results for the business.
- Decide how to allocate the necessary resources and efforts to produce the desired extraordinary results.
- Determine how to redirect resources from areas of low (diminishing) results to areas of high (increasing) results.
- Consider which activities should be abandoned, to be able to invest more money in future opportunities (activities).

These five optimization decisions must first and foremost focus on; effectiveness in producing revenue, creating markets, and developing the appropriate products, services and markets. As we have emphasized throughout this Mini MBA, effectiveness is critical for every business however, we should also remember that even the most effective businesses can die due to poor efficiency, especially if that business is efficient in doing the wrong things. Therefore, effectiveness is the foundation of success, but efficiency is a minimum condition for survival.

TASK: Drucker Tasks Audit

Before reading any further, now take a moment to note down what might be the **priorities and actions** (for each manager task), based on your current role in your organization (using the Drucker Task Audit framework).

Drucker Tasks Audit

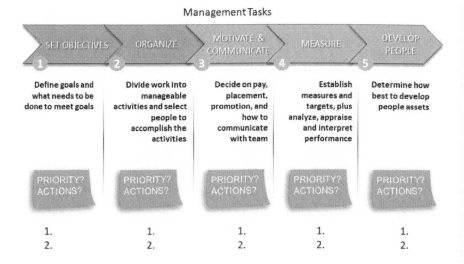

Management Tasks

SET OBJECTIVES	ORGANIZE	MOTIVATE & COMMUNICATE	MEASURE	DEVELOP PEOPLE
1	2	3	4	5
Define goals and what needs to be done to meet goals	Divide work into manageable activities and select people to accomplish the activities	Decide on pay, placement, promotion, and how to communicate with team	Establish measures and targets, plus analyze, appraise and interpret performance	Determine how best to develop people assets
PRIORITY? ACTIONS?	PRIORITY? ACTIONS?	PRIORITY? ACTIONS?	PRIORITY? ACTIONS?	PRIORITY? ACTIONS?
1. 2.	1. 2.	1. 2.	1. 2.	1. 2.

Drucker, P. (2006). The Effective Executive

Making Decisions

One of the most important decisions a manager makes every day is; where to invest time and effort? This is a critical because, it is a well-known fact that in most businesses only 10% or 20% of the inputs & processes (products, orders, customers, markets, or people), produce 80% to 90% of the results. What this means is that management must focus on those very few core or worthwhile activities which are in fact capable of being the most effective. Managers should do this because; by doing so they can help bring the business closer to the full realization of its potential. Focusing is critically important. It is important because most businesses operate at a low level of performance when they are measured against their optimal potential. To avoid this sub-optimization, managers should constantly ask the following three questions;

1. What is the theoretical optimum level of performance for my business?
2. What is preventing us from achieving that optimum level?
3. What are the limiting factors (bottlenecks) which are holding us back from achieving the theoretical optimum level of performance (based on resources and effort made)?

Because of the unique nature of every company, and the business environments they operate in. The answers to the three optimization questions will be different for every industry, business, and functional area.

DRILL 5: Summary

1. Management is about doing things right, and Leadership is about doing the right things.
2. There are five primary tasks of a manager;
   a. Setting objectives.
   b. Organizing.
   c. Motivating and communicating.
   d. Measuring performance.
   e. Developing people.

3. Business performance comes first, because performance is the aim of the enterprise and the reason for its existence. Without good performance, companies are unable to contribute to societal issues and to build a future for their business.

TASK: Leadership Traits

Everything you need to know about management you can still learn from reading Peter Drucker. Drucker viewed leadership in terms of performance and effectiveness (true for both CEOs and middle managers). Rick Wartzman, executive director of The Drucker Institute at Claremont Graduate University, created a checklist against which companies could measure themselves (based on Drucker's Principles). Go through the checklist and evaluate how your organization ranks on these criteria.

LINK: The Ten Traits of a Drucker-like Manager
https://goo.gl/9x9Hhl

SOURCES:

Drucker, P. (2006). The Effective Executive. Harper Collins

Charan, R., Barton, D., & Carey, D. (2015). People Before Strategy: A New Role for the CHRO. Harvard Business Review

DRILL 6: Decision Making

'The only easy day was yesterday' ~ Navy SEAL

According to Professor Ron Howard (Stanford University), 'A good decision never turns into a bad decision, and a bad decision never turns into a good decision'. That is a wise thing to remember for us all because, managers are paid to make decisions and will be judged on their success rate from those decisions. Therefore, it is important to learn good decision-making practices. In this Mini MBA drill, we will focus on three tools which can help in making better decisions. The first tool will help in managing ones' time. The second tool helps define real problems and challenges. The third tool helps to make better decisions.

TOOL 1: TIME MANAGET GRID (TMG)

The TMG helps set priorities. Setting priorities is important, because managers live in a time-pressured world. Therefore, it is not uncommon for managers to have overlapping commitments which require immediate attention. In other words, the commitments all appear to be urgent right now! Urgency is an everyday occurrence for most managers, but missing deadlines is not a path to advancing ones' career. Therefore, based on urgent conditions and the need to make decisions, how can a manager balance the flood of responsibilities, achieve excellent work and maintain a healthy state of mind? TMG can help organize and prioritize overlapping commitments.

The TMG analysis helps to categorize decisions and tasks which should be addressed. The TMG analysis is based on two criteria, which are further divided up into four quadrants. The two criteria are decision importance and decision urgency.

Urgent vs Important

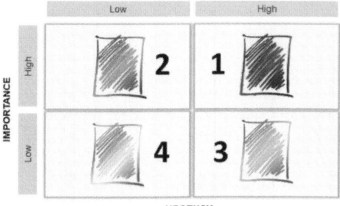

- **Quadrant one** in the TMG is filled with items that are urgent and important. This means that items in this quadrant are the most pressing decisions (meetings, deadlines etc.) which should have been done yesterday? Items placed in quadrant one can be the cause of a crisis or major problem. Therefore, those items should never be neglected.
- **Quadrant two** items are not urgent but are important. These are things that matter in the long-term but will not benefit from immediate attention. Quadrant two items can be delayed, but should not be neglected for too long.
- **Quadrant three** items are urgent but not important. For most managers, quadrant three is filled with things that take up a lot of time but are often a waste of time and could be avoided. Avoiding these will free up time for more urgent and important matters. When creating a personal TMG, pay attention to this quadrant, especially when trying to find more time for urgent and important matters.
- **Quadrant four** items are not urgent and not important. These are things we often do when we are tired or need a break. They are major cause of wasted work time.

Management is about prioritizing time and attention. However, to do that effectively, one must first determine what is most important to deal with in the first place. The challenge is that everything appears to be urgent and important. But, if one is honest, one can always find items which could put into TMG quadrants three and four. The benefit of completing a TMG analysis is that it can helps achieve more focus on vital issues which require attention now! Furthermore, TMG helps avoid those everyday distractions which consume a great deal of valuable time!

Completing The TMG

It is now time to complete your TMG. Before doing so, make a list of ten (or more) activities or decisions which need to be dealt with (important and urgent). Place each of those items into one of the four TMG quadrants. If you have difficulty finding items for quadrant three or four, force yourself to switch some items from quadrants one or two into quadrants three and four.

LINK: TMG GRID Analysis Sheet **(pdf)**
https://goo.gl/GoqS1d

Urgent vs. Important Matrix

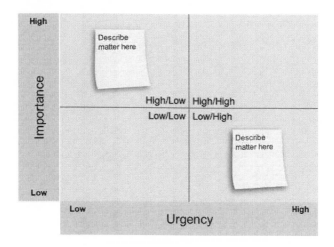

The results from completing this simple TMG exercise should allow you to define the most important things you should be doing first. By doing just that, the TMG helps you focus-in on the most important/urgent priorities you are currently facing. A disciplined TMG analysis is the first step towards better decision making.

TOOL 2: THE 5 WHYS

5 Whys helps identify real problems (root cause analysis). The history of 5 Whys dates to the 1930's and Sakichi Toyoda (founder of Toyota Industries). Toyota managers still use the 5 Whys to solve problems every day. The 5 Whys at first appears to be very simple because, when faced with a problem one simply asks 5 times; why did that problem occur? However, only by practicing the process can one master its power. 5 Whys is based upon the Toyota Go and See philosophy;

'Gaining an in-depth understanding of the systems, processes and conditions of a problem, where ever it may have occurred, is much more effective than just reflecting from a distance on what might have happened.'

Identify the root cause of a problem is necessary before fixing a problem. Here is an example of how Toyota uses 5 Whys. Imagine for a moment that one of Toyota's assembly line robots has stopped. When this occurs, the Toyota manager responsible for the robot line would begin to apply the 5 Whys tool by asking;

1. **Why did the robot stop?**
   ✓ *The answer the manager might arrive at could be, 'It stopped because an electronic circuit overloaded'. The manager then asks;*

2. **Why did the circuit overload?**
   ✓ *'The circuit overloaded because there was not enough lubrication on the bearings, and they locked up'.*
3. **Why was there not enough lubricant on the bearings?**

✓ *'The oil pump on the robot is not circulating enough oil'.*
4. **Why is the pump not circulating enough oil?**
   ✓ *'Because the pump intake is blocked with small metal pieces which fall in from the manufacturing processes'.*
5. **Why is the pump intake blocked with small metal pieces?**
   ✓ *'Because there is no filter on the pump'*

Based on this questioning process, the root-cause of the robot stopping can be identified;

'There was no filter on the pump'

The 5 Whys can help in identifying the root cause of almost any problem. However, one must remember that each why must be looking for an answer that is grounded in fact. Furthermore, the answer to each why must be an account of things that have happened, and not just events that might have happened. In addition, one must keep asking why until they feel confident that they have identified the root-cause. This is necessary because when one reaches that final why point, they can go no further. After identifying the root-cause (the 5th why), the underlying causes (processes) should become evident. Only then can one decide on the action to be taken.

Completing The 5 Whys

It is now time to complete a 5 Whys analysis. Before doing so, identify a problem that needs to be dealt with. For that problem, go through each Why. When doing so, also consider what system failures might have contributed to the problem. If you have difficulty progressing beyond the first or second Why, ask someone to work with you. Furthermore, consider the following during each stage;

- Causes of each different why situation.
- Reasons the problem was not identified in the first place.
- System failures (do not only question processes).

5 Whys – Root-Cause Analysis

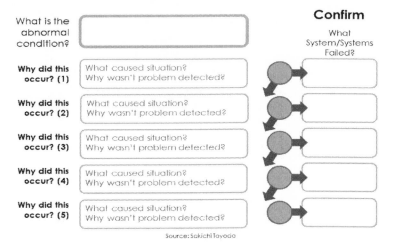

Source: Sakichi Toyoda

Keep in mind that the 5 Whys are more suited to less complicated or moderately-difficult problems. Complex problems on the other hand, require a more detailed approach to the problem. However, almost any problem can benefit from applying Sakichi Toyoda's 5 Whys.

TOOL 3: STANFORD DECISION-CHAIN

According to research at Stanford University, only 2% of managers have been found to regularly apply best practices when making decisions. Nobody wants to be one of those 98% of managers who do not apply best practices? Using the decision chain can increase the number of good business decisions you made and help improve decision quality. However, when using this tool, it's important to remember that each link is inter-connected with all other links (this is not a linear process). What this means is that each decision made, when going through the chain, has an impact on previous and future decisions. Now lest say a few words about each of the six links in the chain.

#1: Correct Framework

The first link is called the correct framework. What this means is that when working on the right decisions everyone is;

- Clear about the purpose.
- Have defined the scope or boundaries of that decision.
- Are aware of each person's point of view (rational that is being brought to the decision).
- Solving the decision in the right way, and with the involvement of others.

#2: Correct Alternatives

Correct alternatives make sure that we have considered creative and doable alternatives. This is because, if those alternatives are not doable, we can't make them happen. Furthermore, the alternatives should be significantly different from each other.

#3: Right Information

Right information helps us to be more confident in the decision we will make. However, for this to happen, the information we use must be forward looking and involve some uncertainty. Because of these factors (forward looking and uncertainty) it is essential we use relevant and trusted information (judge if that information is good or bad).

#4: Clear Goals

Clear goals help us focus on value creation when choosing our alternatives. To do that, we must define the value metrics we are using, in addition to their benefits and weaknesses.

#5: Proper Reasoning

Proper reasoning helps us to determine which alternatives give us the most of what we want. However, the challenge is to make sure that we are using the correct decision logic, and to also consider any uncertainties which might exist. In addition, remember to break down the complexity of the decision into smaller pieces, because only by doing this can we arrive at clear choices.

The first five links in the decision chain help to create clarity on what is necessary to know to decide (our intentions). However, remember that intention is not the same as action, and this leads us to the sixth link in the decision chain.

#6: Commitment to Action

Commitment to action is important to remember because; decisions are not really made until resources have been allocated to deal with the issues identified. Therefore, being committed to action requires people to make a shift from thinking-to doing. When making this shift, all conflicts between people must be identified and resolved then and there. More importantly, the involvement of people who will implement the decisions, and make them happen, must also be established.

The Decision Chain

Each Steps Is Inter-Connected
All 6 issues rank as close to 100% as possible before decision is made.

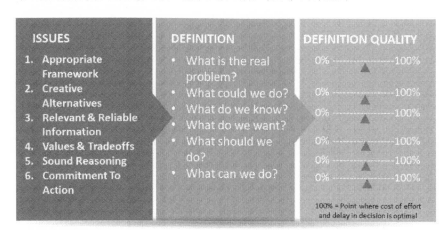

Source: Stanford Strategic Decision & Risk Management

The six links in the Decision Chain represent a more systematic way to consider all the decision requirements needed, to make quality decisions.

DRILL 6: Summary

1. When completing the TMG, force yourself to switch some items from quadrants one or two into quadrants three and four.
2. Identify the root cause of a problem is necessary before fixing a problem.
3. The six links in the Stanford Decision Chain represent a more systematic way to consider all the decision requirements needed, to make quality decisions.

TASK: Decision Inventory

This self-assessment inventory describes how you go about making important decisions.

LINK: Decision Style Inventory
https://goo.gl/juQS9X
Note: No registration is required to complete inventory

SOURCES:

Covey, S. (1989). The Seven Habits of Highly Effective People. Free Press

Semler, R. (2004). The Seven Day Weekend. Penguin

Spetzler, C., Winter, H., & Meyer, J. (2016). Decision Quality: Value Creation for Better Decision Making. Strategic Decision Group International

Allinson, C.W., & Hayes, J. (1996). The Cognitive Style Index: A Measure of Intuition-Analysis for Organizational Research, Journal of Management Studies

DRILL 7: Economics

Pricing The iPhone?

Let's begin this drill by imagining that we are stepping into a time machine. In this time machine, we will be transported back to the year 2007 and we land in Cupertino California at Apple Corporation. Apple is just about to launch the first iPhone, and we will be one of the managers responsible for the iPhone launch. One of the most important things which need to be decided is the price of that first iPhone? How should we decide that price?

The standard economic and rational approach to setting the price for the first iPhone would be is as follows;

- Ask focus groups about various price points for the iPhone phone.
- Based on those findings, pick the price 'management think' could maximize profits (say that price was $400).

Neo-Classical Economics

We will come back to this pricing decision in just a moment. However, some additional information about what was occurring just around the time of the pricing decision might be helpful at this stage. On October of that same year Alan Greenspan, who was the former Chairman of the U.S. Federal Reserve Bank and considered to be the greatest banker who ever lived, confessed that he was shocked. Greenspan was shocked because the financial markets had not operated as he had expected. That October, Greenspan admitted that he had 'made a mistake in assuming those banks and other financial institutions were capable of protecting shareholders'. He even confessed that his belief in the rationality of markets, organizations, and people had fallen apart. What Greenspan was saying was that markets were not always capable of making rational decisions, and not always healthily self-regulating institutions.

The Invisible Hand

This statement may not sound very important but in fact it was totally opposite to the conventional economic thinking of the time. The thinking of that time was built upon the principal of 'The Invisible Hand'. However, Greenspan was admitting that the invisible hand might in fact be irrational. This might already sound like economy-speak, but in fact, the principal of the invisible hand (first used by Adam Smith in 1759) stated that 'individuals' (or firms) efforts to pursue their own interests may frequently benefit society more than if their actions were directly intending to benefit society'! What Smith meant was that markets automatically channel self-interest toward socially desirable ends. However, the financial earthquake of 2008, along with Chairman Greenspan's comments, brought into question the validity of all classical economic thinking and the invisible hand principle.

This is very important to understand in this Bootcamp drill because the invisible hand is probably the single most important proposition ever made in economic theory. However, today more than ever, economists are beginning to question if in fact competitive markets truly do a good job at allocating resources, and if not, what is the proper balance between markets and governments? Now let's fast-forward to the present time, and what we see emerging is an outright questioning of economics as it has been taught in business schools for the past 100 years. Therefore, even business school economists are questioning if in fact human beings and markets are rational, and if they are not, how does irrationality drive human decision making? More importantly, if human decision making is irrational, how should business managers run their businesses and make decisions (pricing the iPhone for example)?

At the time Apple was deciding on the iPhone pricing decision, economics was all about studying how nations, companies and people (agents) use scarce resources to satisfy unlimited wants (neo-classical economics). There were two primary branches of economics being practiced (macroeconomics and microeconomics). Macroeconomics concerned itself with large scale market systems, and the performance, structure and behavior of economies. Microeconomics is more focused on the choices made by individual actors (firms or individual consumers). The point here is that the distinction between these two branches of economics (macro and micro) were already becoming blurred at that time.

Furthermore, for 100 years or more, business schools had been teaching neoclassical economic thinking (Micro and Macro). This way thinking promoted the idea that; the only duty of MBA's should be to 'maximize shareholder value'. This 'profit maximization' principal in fact formed an important part of neoclassical economic thinking and assumed that; 'companies and individuals have rational expectations to maximize their tastes or preferences'. To put this more simply, we are all rational!

Neoclassical economic thinking also presumed that people act independently based on all the information they can gather. Based on this presumption; markets are always in balance. However, the failure of financial markets throughout the world in 2008 called into question the neoclassical school of thinking, which had guided markets for more than 100 years. Despite what one might think thinking, even after the financial earthquake of 2008, the neoclassical way of thinking is still powerful. One could even say it is 'how the world works today'. Therefore, rationally motivated behavior is still used to make predictions about the quantity of goods that get produced and the prices at which they will be sold. However, some enlightened thought has emerged, even within business economics circles. This enlightened thought has even gone so far as to suggest that; when we teach MBA student's economics, we should also emphasize the importance of avoiding profit-maximizing activities that may harm society at large.

Pricing The iPhone

According to the neoclassical view; consumers, workers, and companies make rational calculations about what is in their own best interests. However, if in fact we are not all rationally motivated what does this mean for managers who are making important decisions? To help us consider this matter, let's now return to the time machine and re-visit Cupertino California on the day of the first iPhone release. On June 29th, 2007, Apple introduced the iPhone at a price-point of $600. However, very soon after the launch, Apple quickly reduced the price to $400, which was the rational price arrived at in our earlier discussion. The important question for us is; 'Why did Apple do this'?

Well, Apple made that decision because they used an alternative approach to pricing the first iPhone. By alternative, we mean that Apple was not only following the principles of neoclassical economics (rational decision making). In fact, their novel approach to pricing was based on a combined neo-classical and behavioral approach to pricing the iPhone. This combined process might have gone something like the following;

- Apple management questioned all assumptions such as; do people know how to value a revolutionary new product.
- Apple management designed different pricing experiments.
- Apple determined the optimal price from those experiments ($400).

- Apple also tried to discover how people might arrive at a decision to buy the product. Based on that finding, they considered again the optimal price for the iPhone.
- Apple then considered how a launch price of $600 might influence 'the perception of value' for the iPhone over a longer period?

Based on this process, Apple decided to launch at $600. By launching the iPhone at $600, Apple was in fact able to make consumers think later that, $400 was a bargain! Furthermore, if Apple had launched the iPhone at $400, consumers would never have had the possibility to compare prices. This is an important point to remember in this case because; consumers had never seen a product like the iPhone before. The alternative approach to pricing the iPhone took this into account because Apple management also considered how people make decisions.

Behavioural Economics

Therefore, unlike neoclassical economic thinking, the behavioral approach to pricing the iPhone meant that Apple also considered the roles of buyer habit, trust, and other consumer choice behaviors. The word 'behavior' is important to understand in this context because it is a reminder that there is something going on in the mind of the consumer, and this something had been previously neglected by neo-classical economists. To confirm this important point, recent developments in brain imaging technology have now allowed managers to enter the minds of consumers, and observe decision making processes. For example, Prof. Jonathan Cohen (Princeton University), has completed brain imaging studies which show that often, human decision making involves brain mechanisms that are associated with emotional responses (not only rational analysis). Dr. Cohen's research findings confirm that emotions play a very important role in consumer decision making. This is an important, point because managers need to better understand how emotions influence behavior and decision making.

However, despite the findings of Prof. Cohen and other researchers in his field, and although most economists are willing to accept these findings (human decisions are often reached emotionally), most economists continue to preach the neoclassical message (firms and individuals make a rational calculation as to what is in their own best interests).

So, what exactly is behavioral economics? Well, unlike neo-classical economics, behavioral economics is primarily concerned with the limits of economic agents (companies and people). In simple English, the term 'limits of economic agents' mean that when people make decisions, their rationality is limited by;

- The available information.
- The ability to manage the decision problem faced.
- The cognitive limitations (knowledge and understanding) of the mind.
- The time available (un-available) when to make decisions.

Reflecting on the 2008 worldwide financial earthquake and Chairman Greenspan's comments, it is no wonder that behavioral economics is increasingly discussed as a valuable alternative to neoclassical economics. Furthermore, one might also say that managers would benefit considerably from taking a more experimental approach to decision making, based on behavioral economic thinking. This is the case because; behavioral experiments can get to the bottom of people's decisions and resulting actions. However, we shouldn't forget that traditional business experiments can also be beneficial. Unfortunately, traditional experiments are often like engineering projects which built around established governing principles, and those principles are driven by;

- Assumptions made about the laws that govern behavior.
- Experiments which are based on those limiting assumptions.

However, unlike the engineering approach, behavioral experimentation is more like a science project. This is because, behavioral economists are searching for both the governing principles in decision making along with ways to implement those principles. The challenge with this alternative approach is how can businesses build behavioral thinking into their decision-making processes? Building this capability is important because behavioral experiments have demonstrated that human beings are incapable of making good decisions, they are emotional, easily confused and distracted. Therefore, taking an alternative approach to market research could in fact help improve managerial decision making and reduce the risk of the decisions made.

According to Professor Dan Ariely (Duke University), by taking a behavioral approach, managers could in fact improve decision making and lessen the risk. Prof. Ariely recommends that smart organizations must begin to develop 'behavioral economics capabilities' and start practicing those capabilities with small experiments. However, Prof. Ariely also reminds us that management often involves a mixture of situations, many of which are repeated. In repetitive cases, experience-based intuition is still valuable. However, when we encounter unknown (uncertain) situations a manager's intuition might be of no value at all, if not dangerous. Therefore, part of the appeal of the behavioral approach to research is that it could add value. A more behavioral approach could add value because 'even if the results don't define what to do, they will prevent anyone from thinking in the wrong way. Prof. Ariely makes an important point; the goal should always be to make more informed decisions.

DRILL 7: Summary

1. Adam Smith's Invisible Hand: Markets automatically channel self-interest toward socially desirable ends.
2. Neoclassical economic thinking presumed that people act independently based on all the information they can gather therefore; markets are always in balance.
3. Behavioral economics is concerned with the limits of economic agents (companies and people). When people make decisions, their rationality is limited.

TASK: How Rational Are You?

This assessment identifies which of 16 reasoning styles you use, where your reasoning strengths lie, and what you can do to improve your reasoning skills. It will also tell you what your overall level of rationality is!

LINK: How rational Are You Really
https://goo.gl/5u2lL3
Note: Registration is required to view quiz results. However, the results are quite detailed and informative.

SOURCES:

Chang, H-J. (2014). Economics: The User's Guide. Bloomsbury Press

Ariely, D., & Samson, A. (2015). The Behavioral Economics Guide 2015

Thaler, R. (2015). Misbehaving: The Making of Behavioral Economics

Cox, J. (2007). The Concise Guide to Economics

Ariely, D. (2011). The Upside of Irrationality

DRILL 8: Finance

'It pays to be a winner' ~ Navy SEAL

Value Creation

If one believes in the old saying 'it takes money to make money,' then one already understands that cash flow is important to every company and manager. The cash flow statement of a company in fact reveals how a company spends its money (cash outflows) and where that money comes from (cash inflows). During the economics drill we raised the important issue of shareholder value and we also discussed how 'the single pursuit by managers to increase shareholder value, might in fact be the cause of a lot of the economic problems we face today. However, Professor Alfred Rappaport (The Kellogg School of Management, Northwestern University) would not necessarily agree with that statement. In Alfred's opinion, the reality is that the shareholder value principle has not failed management; rather it is 'management that has betrayed the principle of shareholder value'. The real challenge is we should learn to appreciate a simpler definition of value. In this drill, we will learn more about that definition.

At its most basic level, the value of a business is the sum of the present value of future expected cash flow. Present value is the value now of a sum of money, and that value is very different from some future value a sum of money will have (after compound interest rates or returns from investments made with the present money available.). In Alfred's simple definition, a company's value has four major components which are based on;

1. Who is managing the company and their strategy?
2. The stock price (driven by the expectations of the market).
3. The ability to invest capital at a higher rate of return (ROC), than the cost of capital.
4. Generating higher cash flows.

Every manager would be wise to focus on these four value principles, because misunderstanding 'value' has caused a lot of companies to miss opportunities to create long-term value.

Definitions

Before beginning a Mini-Case on Amazon Corporation, let's first define some critical terms which will come up in that case. The first term is shareholder value. A common definition of shareholder value is; the extent to which it enriches shareholders. The second term we need to understand is operating cash flow (OCF). OCF measures the amount of cash generated by a company's normal business operations. Next, we need to understand free cash flow (FCF). FCF is the measure of a company's financial performance and is calculated as; operating cash flow minus capital expenditures. Then we have net income (total earnings), which is defined as; revenues minus the costs of doing business (such as depreciation, interest, taxes and other expenses). Finally, we have the cash conversion cycle (CCC). The CCC expresses the length of time (days) that it takes for a company to convert resource inputs into cash flows. Therefore, CCC measures the amount of time needed to sell inventory, collect receivables, along with the length of time to pay bills (without incurring penalties).

MINI-CASE: Amazon Marketplace

Amazon management are not very interested in 'shareholder value'. By saying this, we mean that Amazon management, at least in the traditional sense of value as practiced by many companies, is not following that rule. Jeff Bezos, the founder of Amazon and the third richest person in the world, has understood from the beginning that the meaning of real value in a business is not just about shareholder value. Therefore, Jeff and his team at Amazon are much more, focused on, cash flow. Furthermore, in the immediate future, Amazon is, unlikely to start focusing on shareholder 'value' (in the traditional sense).

Financial History of Amazon

Why is Amazon not particularly interested in shareholder value? To understand the origin of this principle we need to go back into the history of Amazon. Since May 15th, 1997 (the day Amazon went public), investors have in fact complained about Amazon's unprofitable business performance. Many people even thought that the Amazon business model was broken. However, despite this criticism, Jeff and the management of Amazon have continued to grow revenues every year without ever making a profit (Amazon did make a small profit in 2016).

What was the secret that allowed Amazon to grow rapidly, but not make any profit? The Amazon's secret was that they have been focused on re-investing a very healthy cash flow on growing revenues rapidly and developing the business even further. What this means is that Amazon is a cash flow funded growth machine. That growth has also allowed Amazon to offer the lowest prices, and to create more customer loyalty, which has helped to power their growth.

Therefore, distributing profits to shareholders has been a secondary concern for the management of Amazon. This is because; revenue (and the resulting cash flow) is their primary concern. This is a principle which Amazon management has understood better than most others. In fact, for Amazon 'increasing profitability would slow down that growth'. Think about that statement for a moment 'increasing profitability would slow down growth'. In fact, that statement is totally opposite to neo-classical economic principles. This is because, for neoclassical economists 'the goal of every company should be profit maximization'. However, for Amazon the primary goal is continuous growth (as rapid as possible)! Furthermore, one critical component of that growth is the management of cash flow.

Cash Flow at Amazon

So, what does cash flow look like at Amazon? Operating cash flow (OCF) was almost $9 Billion in 2015 and has been growing exponentially over the years. Free cash flow (FCF) was $4.4 Bn. (very healthy). However, net income has been very disappointing for the market. Now let's peek under the hood of this cash flow machine. First is the matter of net income. Amazon calculate net income in the following way; when Amazon sell a book online, the money received from the buyer and the money paid out to the publisher (or supplier) of the book are recorded in the same time-period. This is done, even though the payments to the publishers don't happen at the same time. This gap in fact is very important for the Amazon cash flow machine.

Free cash flow (FCF) at Amazon is calculated when money changes hands. What this means is that when a customer pays quickly, and if Amazon manage their inventory well, they take their time in paying the publishers. Because of this lag, free cash flow is positive and very healthy, even when net income is not. This simple transaction process is one of the primary reasons for the excellent performance of the Amazon business model (growth). According to Professor Mihir Desai (Harvard Business School), the key Amazon metric for generating cash is the cash conversion cycle (CCC). The CCC is defined as: days of inventory + days sales outstanding. In other words, how long it takes the Amazon customer to pay; minus how many days it takes Amazon to pay their suppliers (publishers etc.).

Benchmarking Amazon

How does Amazon cash flow management compare with other retailers (Walmart and Costco)? Walmart and Costco have single digit CCC's (quite impressive). However, Amazon has a CCC of -33 days. That CCC figure is unbelievable, and very few companies can achieve those levels, other than Apple Corporation (-44). What a CCC of -33 days means is that Amazon and Apple are cash flow machines. For Amazon, all that excess cash is used to finance growth (the real value of their business). Furthermore, Amazon has no need to borrow money, issue more stock (equity) or to raise money. This means Amazon can keep using their own cash to develop new businesses, and to upgrade current offerings. Professor Desai (Harvard Business School) describes Amazon as an 'excellent case of a company that has an economically fine-tuned engine which effectively serves their goal in a really interesting and thoughtful way', if their future investments pay-off. The excessive free cash flow at Amazon also makes it possible to experiment, learn from those mistakes, and keep moving ahead, regardless of what shareholders think.

Inventory Management at Amazon

In the Amazon model, great inventory management does also matter. So, how great is Amazon at inventory management? That's a good question. To understand how Amazon performs on inventory management, we need to understand the concept of inventory velocity. Inventory velocity is measured as; the point when Amazon collect cash from customers, compared to the point when they pay suppliers. Based on this inventory velocity formula, Amazon is not an inventory velocity champion. As a matter of fact, Walmart and Amazon have almost the same inventory velocity, and Costco turns its inventory much faster. Furthermore, customers pay Walmart and Costco faster than Amazon's customers do! However, here is the key point which makes inventory velocity less important to Amazon. Amazon takes a very long time to pay their suppliers! In fact, they take almost 97 days on average to pay suppliers, compared to Walmart (38), and Costco (30). It goes without saying that, 97-day payment terms are amazing. In fact, observers are beginning to wonder; how long will suppliers to Amazon put up with that?

The business model at Amazon is of course also dependent upon continuous growth. Therefore, a critical question is; what is the growth potential of Amazon? The answer to this question is best understood by looking at the retail sector in general. Amazon currently has around 1% to 2% of the total US retail market (in terms of value). Therefore, based on this low market share figure, there is considerable scope for growth, even within their existing markets. Jeff Bezos and his excellent management team seem to have a clear view on what they are planning to do in the future;

- Continue to identify new growth opportunities.
- Continue to re-invest profits into the business.
- Continue to use 'every single last penny' to do that.

DRILL 8: Summary

1. The principal of value says that;
   a. Excellent strategy and management are essential to create value.
   b. Market expectations have an impact on value (but value creation means more than just market expectations).
   c. Managers must work towards achieving a rate of return (ROC), greater than the cost of money needed to fund growth.
   d. Maximizing cash flow generates cash to fund future growth because;
2. Free cash flow can be improved by: getting customers to pay quickly, managing inventory well, and taking as much time as the market will bear, to pay suppliers. By following this rule, a company's free cash flow will become more attractive, even if net income is not.
3. Healthy free-cash flow means a company can experiment, learn from mistakes, and keep moving ahead. Free cash flow increases the value of a business.

THE BAD NEWS!

The overriding assumption in this discussion has been that; most companies are investing for the future. However, the data shows us that this is not necessarily the case. According to Professor William Lazonick (University of Massachusetts), instead of creating value for their firms, Top executives of firms have in fact, through the massive use of share-buybacks, extracted value. Prof. Lazonick discovered in his research that between 2003 and 2012, publicly-listed firms on the US S&P 500 (500 largest listed companies) used 94% percent of their profits ($2.4 trillion dollars) to buy back their own stock or pay-out dividends. Those transactions transferred large profits to shareholder activists. What this means is that 94% of profits added no gain to the companies.

This practice has not always been the case. For example, from 1945 to the late 1970s, the dominant approach by companies was to retain profits and reinvest those profits into their businesses. During that period firms 'retained earnings and reinvested them to increase their capabilities'. However, from the late 1970s to the present day, the focus has been on reducing costs and distributing the freed-up cash to financial interests (shareholders).

Prof. Lazonick says that the root cause of this problem is the philosophy of 'maximizing shareholder value'. Furthermore, he says that with 94% of earnings going to share buybacks and dividends, there are only 6% of the profits left to re-invest for the future of those businesses. Therefore, be aware of the realities of how markets really work. One might even say that; irrationality after all is not in short supply, especially if we consider the future viability of every business.

TASK: Cash Flow Tutorials

These videos will help you better understand cash flow and the cash flow statement.

VIDEO LINK: What is Cash Flow
https://goo.gl/YWAQ55

VIDEO LINK: The Cash Flow Statement
https://goo.gl/BXLTbt

Note: The video links bring you to the Dr. G.L. Danford video library.

SOURCES:

Koller, T., Dobbs, R., & Huyett, B. (2010). Value: The Four Cornerstones of Corporate Finance. McKinsey and Co.

Ackman, W. (2012). Everything You Need to Know About Finance. Big Think

Schiff, P. (2014). Myths Maximizing Shareholder Value

Lazonick, W. (2014). Profit Without Prosperity. Harvard Business Review

Desai, M. (2014). At Amazon, It's All About Cash Flow. Harvard Business Review

Loth, R. Analyze Cash Flow the Easy Way. Investopedia

DRILL 9: Accounting

'Focus only on high value targets' ~ Navy SEAL

Moneyball

Money Ball is a movie about Billy Beane (played by Brad Pitt). Beane is General Manager of the Oakland A's, a professional baseball team in the US. In the movie the Oakland A's are losing all their star players to other clubs, and Beane's challenge is to try and put together a competitive team for the upcoming season. The challenge for Beane is that Oakland has a limited payroll (money) to attract new star players. Early in the movie, Beane accidently meets a Yale University economics graduate called Peter Brand (played by Johan Hill). Peter has some crazy ideas about how to identify potential new players for the team, based on a statistical model of player data he created (algorithm). The number one statistic measured in the model is; on-base-percentage (OBP). OBP calculates how often a batter reaches first base.

Before US teams started using OBT, they sent out scouts who traveled around the country trying to identify junior players with potential. This scout system selection process was based mostly on subjective criteria (what the scout thought about a player's potential). However, Peter's statistical model proved to be a more effective measure for evaluating potential player's along with overall team performance. In the following season, Oakland won most of their games, and went on to play the Baseball World Series, just because of the OBT algorithm.

What is the main point in this 'Money Ball' story? The main point is that; what gets measured gets done. Therefore, the main purpose of accounting information for managers should be to help make better decisions. Like in the Money Ball movie, by following this rule, your company can also become a champion.

Key Performance Indicators (KPI's)

Therefore, the accounting information gathered in a company must provide managers with the data needed to effectively operate their business. Furthermore, accounting information should measure business transactions which help steer managers in the right direction. This is a better approach than making decisions based on only gut-feelings, like the scouts were doing in the Money Ball movie. Moreover, managers should always have key metrics (measures) available, which shows them the progress being made towards the desired outcomes, and the gaps between the actual and targeted performance. In business we often refer to these measures as Key Performance Indicators (KPI's). However, it is essential to have good KPI's;

- Objective measures (not just based on gut-feelings).
- Comparable to previous data, and the desired performance.
- Focus people's attention on what really matters to achieve success.
- Measure accomplishments, and not just the work done.
- Become the common language for communication.
- Help reduce uncertainty.
- Measure the right things.
- Can be verified and proven to be accurate.

However, it can be very difficult to define meaningful KPI's. This is difficult because valuable KPI's are different for every business, every company, and every business function (production, finance, marketing etc.). Therefore, the concept of KPI's is easy to understand, but identifying, measuring, monitoring and validating the best KPI's for a business, or functional area, can be a very difficult challenge. Furthermore, there should not be too many KPI's.

Context-specific KPI's

To illustrate the differences in KPI's, imagine a manager for an online e-commerce business. What might be the critical KPI's which are needed to follow regularly for that kind of e-business? Well, one critical KPI might be conversion rate (how many visitors are converted into customers). An even more critical KPI might be retention (how many people converted remain active customers for a defined period). For a manager in a food retail company on the other hand, a critical KPI might be; sales-per-square-foot (square meter) of shop space. For a customer service manager, a critical KPI might be; average resolution time (how long it takes to solve an individual customer's problem). This list of KPI's by industry, company, and functional area can go on and on (there are 100's of them).

It is essential that the KPI's selected (and monitored) must be ones that are most relevant for a specific company's individual business conditions. However, the challenge then is; how does a manager decide on their unique KPI's? According to the Balanced Scorecard Institute (Harvard Business School), one can determine unique KPI's by following six steps;

1. Define the intended result(s).
2. Understand the alternative measures.
3. Select the right measurement(s) for each goal or objective.
4. Define composite indicators (combine individual measures into a single index).
5. Set targets and thresholds.
6. Define and regularly document the selected performance measures.

Accounting-based KPI's

After following these six steps, it is important then to collect and monitor the performance of those KPI's, analyze the results, draw conclusions, and based on that analysis improve performance. However, not all KPI's are directly related to financial data or to cash flow, because business success can depend on many factors (customer relationships, employee engagement etc.). Therefore, the selection of KPI's should be customized for each individual business case. However, cash flow and other financial numbers can be the source of some important KPI's data. Accounting-based KPI's might include;

- Accounts receivable: The amount of money the company should be getting from customers. This is important because without money, it's hard to run a business. However, just following this KPI is not enough because, the company must also be able to collect that money.
- Inventory KPI's: Inventory KPI's measure the amount of materials held in the business which can be at some point sold or transformed into a final product. However, doing this the inventory can is a cost for the company. Therefore, the company wants to minimize inventory as much as possible, without harming the business.
- Accounts payable KPI's: Accounts payable KPI's measure the sums of money a company needs to give suppliers at some point in the future, for them to purchase/pay for the raw materials or services needed to carry out the business. It is important to remember, that these KPI's evolve over time and are critical to the performance of every business. For example, to increase performance a manager might shorten the accounts receivables turnover to thirty days and extend payable turnover to sixty days. This action can generate extra liquidity for their business (customers are financing your business operations in the short-term).
- Amazon is an excellent example of this form of KPI management. Amazon gets their money from buyers quite fast but, they take a considerable amount of time to pay the suppliers (sometimes up to ninety days).

Smart KPI's

How can a manager determine the relevance or usefulness of individual KPI's for their business? That is a very good question. One answer to this question is to use the S.M.A.R.T. criteria. SMART criteria help to evaluate the relevance of individual KPI's and each KPI selected should stand up to the following test;

- S = Is the KPI specific?
- M = Is the KPI measurable?
- A = Is the KPI attainable (can it be achieved)?
- R = Is the KPI relevant?
- T = Is the KPI selected time-bound (does time impact it or is the KPI useful over a longer period)?

Planning, Budgeting and Forecasting (PBF)

To conclude this drill on Accounting, we can now say something about; planning, budgeting and forecasting (PBF) because, PBF represents an important function for managers in most companies. According to Deloitte research; PBF is often outdated already when approved. Furthermore, the PBF process in most companies is time-consuming and resource-intensive. In addition to these points, the PBF process is often a finance-focused exercise, with little relevance to managing the company's real core business activities. According to Deloitte, this is because there is a lack of common understanding of the purpose of PBF, and often managers don't fully understand why they are planning forecasting and budgeting, and what PBF should be used for in the first place.

The Six PBF Traps

Therefore, the natural beginning point in any PBF process is to determine the purpose of PBF. When doing this, please remember; the primary purpose during any PBF process should be to execute the strategy, and to gain more cost-consciousness, to understanding and improve decision making. Therefore, the PBF process design should follow from the company's purpose (strategy). The reason that PBF should follow from purpose is that if it does not, one will most likely fall into six traps;

1. There is no strategy is in place.
2. The responsibilities and roles are not clear.
3. There is a lack of business understanding.
4. The PBF models and processes are not adjusted to the purpose.
5. There is a lack of drive and simulation for following the process.
6. The PBF time horizon and frequency have been frozen.

These six points might seem rather obvious however; these six pitfalls are often the cause of failure in most PBF processes. Therefore, the most important thing to remember is that a good PBF process should create value for the company. The PBF process should also be business-oriented, and not just an automatic process, which is reacting to pressure from the finance function. A great PBF process should also help managers make better decisions faster, improve decision-quality and help the company focus of the desired results, rather than just becoming a repetitive analysis of historical data. To understand the six traps better, let's now discuss each, one at a time. This will allow us to better understand how to avoid traps and create value from the PBF process, rather than just creating more work.

1. No Strategy

The first trap has the greatest impact on PBF. That trap is; not having a strategy in place. Often this trap occurs because PBF is ahead of the strategy. This happens because the right strategy has not been put in place. As a result, PBF is not precisely focused on executing the right initiatives or efforts. This matter is important because; a good strategy helps managers understand how they are going to achieve their objectives, and which initiatives or actions are priorities. Therefore, a strategy should form the basis of all PBF activities. This is critical because, a good strategy tells a manager what to focus on (customer acquisition, retaining existing customers, or developing the quality of your companies offering etc.). A good strategy also determines which objectives are most critical for an individual business unit.

2. No Roles and Responsibilities

The second most common trap is that responsibilities and roles have not been made clear. This is often made worse when multiple functions within a business are trying to coordinate PBF goals. The result is that different parties have different timelines. Because of this miss-match, there is no coordination of effort to maximize value. The lesson here is that a company must coordinate their efforts between functions, along with defining the specific roles and responsibilities of everyone involved. This must be done to clearly define who has responsibility for what.

3. No Understanding

The third PBF trap occurs when parties involved in the PBF process do not have a complete understanding of the business being carried out. Without this understanding, PBF ends up 'doing things right, but not doing the right things'. In Deloitte terminology this is called; traditional, optimized and tuned planning. However, if a company wants to be a winner, they should attempt to achieve; dynamic and best-in practice planning because that form of planning is fully integrated with the strategy and with tactical and operational processes.

4. No Purpose

The fourth PBF trap is that the PBF process is not fit-to-purpose. Frequently, the mistake companies make is that one form of PBF process is created, which has been optimized for everyone's purposes. To avoid this trap, a holistic PBF model must be created, along with individual models to serve the business level and individual functions. Furthermore, these models should be focused on what is most important to measure.

5. No Drivers

The fifth PBF trap occurs when companies have not identified the key drivers of their business (KPI'S). Therefore, business unit drivers must be defined (number of support calls, retention etc.), along with the impact of those individual drivers on the business (impact on turnover etc.).

6. Timeline

The sixth PBF trap is that the planning period is often set to the financial timeline, rather than actual business conditions. Because business conditions can vary considerably from a retail shop, to an airplane manufacturer etc. the timeline set must fit those conditions. Therefore, the PBF process should not be planned based only upon the financial calendar and must consider individual business conditions. The most important things to remember from this discussion on PBF is that; the PBF cycle must be based on each company's strategy, and that execution and reporting of results must be focused on priority strategic initiatives.

DRILL 9: Summary

1. The purpose of accounting information is to help make the right decisions (what gets measured gets done). Accounting information can provide managers with some of the data however, other information can support decision making (customer data, market data etc.).
2. Define and gather information on a handful of the key measures which impact your company's performance (KPI'S). These KPI'S help show the progress being made towards achieving the desired outcomes, goals, and the gaps between the actual vs desired performance. Evaluate the relevance of each KPI selected (SMART criteria).
3. There six PBF traps;
   a. Strategy
   b. Responsibilities
   c. Understanding
   d. Purpose
   e. Drivers
   f. Timeline

TASK: The KPI Quiz

This QUIZ will help you to assess your level of knowledge on KPI

LINK: FGConsulting KPI Quiz
https://goo.gl/f8rWO5
Note: No registration is required for the quiz

SOURCES:

Investopedia (2014): Ratio Analysis: Using Financial Ratios

Lewis, M. (2003). Moneyball: The Art of Winning an Unfair Game. W.W. Norton & Company

Guide to Key Performance Indicators (2007). Price Waterhouse Coopers

What Is a Key Performance Indicator (2016). Balanced Scorecard Institute

Doran, G.T. (1981). There's a SMART Way to Write Management's Goals and Objectives. Management Review

Horton, R., Searles, P., & Stone, K. (2014). Integrated Performance Management Plan. Budget. Forecast. Deloitte

Jensby, C.U., Jakobsen, L., & Lundbye, M. (2016). Budgeting and Forecasting: Avoid These Seven Pitfalls. Deloitte

DRILL 10: Marketing

'Anybody want to quit?' ~ Navy SEAL

Marketing Budgets

In this Bootcamp drill we are going to focus on the hard data (numbers, budgets, and activities) which occupy a marketing manager's daily life. We will leave the creative aspects of marketing to the creative people, because they're much better at that! The first hard question we should address is;

What % of our company's budget should be invested in marketing?

That is a challenging question to answer, but to help answer this we only must look at the most recent Forrester research on companies marketing budgets. According to Forrester, B2B firms invest approx. 7.5% to 8.5% of their revenue on marketing, and B2C firms invest from 9.0% to 9.5%. Revenue, for our discussion, could be compared to total sales or turnover. However, some companies might have both B2B and B2C activities, and that makes marketing for them, even more complicated. B2B and B2C are two very different forms of business and could be defined as follows;

- B2B means business-to-business and represents a situation where one business makes a commercial transaction with another business.
- B2C refers to a situation where a business sells products and/or services to end consumers.

One must also remember that marketing investments will go up and down, depending on market conditions and individual company conditions. However, based on the Forrester research findings we could say that; companies in general are investing between 7 1/2 to 9 1/2 cents of every dollar (or Euro) of revenue in marketing. Furthermore, this figure is growing annually at about +4.5% every year worldwide (+12% in USA and UK according to Gartner research). Digital marketing investments are growing faster than any other marketing activity today. This fact is very important for us to understand, and because of this, digital marketing is something we will discuss much more in the next Bootcamp drill, which will focus on digital marketing.

Digital & Traditional Marketing Budgets

Average Increase Overall (by company respondents)

	YEAR			
BUDGET AREA	**2013**	**2014**	**2015**	**2016**
OVERALL	+23%	+26%	+25%	+26%
DIGITAL	+28%	+27%	+27%	+26%
TRADITIONAL	+26%	+28%	+22%	+25%

Source: McKinsey & Company (2015)

Where to Spend Budget?

The next important hard marketing question we might ask is;

How (where) should we spend our marketing budget?

The answer to this question is more challenging because; a company could spend their marketing budget on many different things (advertising, market development etc.). Furthermore, the answer to this question will depend a lot on a company's individual business activities (B2B, B2C, individual products, and services etc.). For the B2B sector, Forrester data does tell us how B2B companies spend their marketing budgets. Based on that data, B2B companies invest over 50% of their marketing budget in just five areas;

1. 14% on shows/conferences/events.
2. 10% on digital marketing & digital advertising.
3. 9% on content marketing (creating and distributing content).
4. 9% on websites.
5. 9% on direct marketing (marketing directly to customers).

In the B2C sector (businesses who markets directly to consumer), it is harder to see how those marketing budgets break down. However, a recent McKinsey consulting 'Global Media Report' does offer some insights into marketing spend for B2C companies. According to McKinsey, digital marketing represented 42% of marketing spend for B2C (that was 10% for B2B). Furthermore, B2C companies spend the largest part of their marketing budgets in traditional marketing channels (almost 60%). These channels include; TV, radio, newspapers, and magazine advertising. According to the McKinsey, the top categories for advertising spend in 2016/2017included;

B2C Advertising Spend
% Budget & Growth Rate (2014-2019) By Area

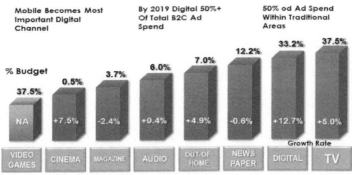

Source: McKinsey & Company (2015)

What this data tells us is that; 50%+ of advertising spend for B2C companies are within traditional areas (TV, newspapers, radio, magazines and cinemas). However, by 2019 digital is expected to represent over 50% of total advertising spend for B2C companies. Furthermore, mobile marketing is expected to become the most important digital marketing platform. Unfortunately, here is where the data begins to get blurred. It gets blurred because increasingly online and off-line marketing are today viewed as one channel by marketers. One reason for this blurring of marketing channel activity is due to the rise of omni-channel, and multi-channel marketing. Omni-channel marketing means that marketers (B2C marketers), are increasingly using at the same time, and with a similar message, multiple channels (for example TV plus mobile, plus social etc.). Multi-channel marketing refers to the optimization of different marketing channels to achieve common goal. This trend towards omni-channel and multi-channel marketing is therefore, creating additional challenges for marketers in all sectors of business.

Mobile Trivia

There were almost 5.7 million car accidents in the United States during 2013 and 27% of all those accidents involved drivers talking or texting on their mobile phones? Therefore, some 1/3 of all car accidents in the US are caused by distracted drivers on their phones. Phones are the #1 reason for car accidents, followed by speeding (#2), drunken driving (#3), or animals (#24). During that year 3,200 people were killed, and 430,000 were injured in their cars because of motor vehicle crashes involving distracted drivers on their cellphones. The point here is that, mobile phones have become increasingly important 8positively and negatively) in all facets of people's lives.

Digital Budget

Coming back to the hard facts on marketing investments by companies, according to McKinsey research, just 4% of digital marketing budgets are directed to mobile in B2C companies. Because this a very important fact for us to remember, let's repeat that number;

- '4% percent of digital marketing budgets are going to mobile marketing activities in B2C companies.'

Therefore, even though mobile accounts for almost 30% of a typical consumer's time spent with media every day (Oracle Corporation research), companies are spending less than 5% of their digital marketing budgets on mobile!

There are lots of opinions on this surprising finding. For example, according to Sir Martin Sorrell (CEO, WPP Group), this 4% spend on mobile is happening because off 'the lack of ability by marketers to measure the impact of their digital advertising'. What Sir Martin is saying is that; marketers don't know if digital advertising works, or if it is worth the money they spend on it. Sir Martin even goes on to say that; under-investment in mobile is due to a lack of clarity around the measurement of mobile advertising, especially within the eco-systems of Facebook and Google. Furthermore, because of this lack of clarity, marketers are still not sure about the return on investment (ROI) of mobile advertising.

This critical statement by Sir Martin Sorell (WPP), that marketers are still not sure about the ROI of mobile advertising, seems to only confirms the old marketing saying; 'half the money I spend on advertising is wasted, the trouble is, I don't know which half.' That saying dates to the 1800's.

Marketing ROI

The third hard data question we could ask about marketing is;

What's the ROI (return on investment) for different marketing channels/activities?

This is in fact the most important and the most challenging question we will address in this Bootcamp drill. To answer that question, we can try to rely on the available data. However, when doing this we should all remember that the data is aggregate (generalized). Therefore, because each company is unique, these data findings are not necessarily the answer to every company's unique marketing situation. However, some data is better than no data at all! So, what is the ROI (return on investment) for different marketing activities?

Measuring ROI

To partially answer the question, we will use the most recent Deloitte, Duke University, and American Marketing Association, 'CMO Study' (CMO is the Chief Marketing Officer of a company, or the highest-ranking marketing executive). Based on those research findings, 'the ability to measure the impact (ROI) of marketing is not very good'. The 2016 research showed that 20% of CMO's can't even prove the impact of marketing and a further 47% percent can only prove some qualitative impact (but it can't be quantified). Therefore, only 33% of CMO's say that they 'can prove the quantitative impact of marketing'.

Return on Advertising Spend (ROAS)

There is some additional data which can help us to understand better marketing ROI. The Advertising Research Foundation (ARF) has been carrying out a cross–industry research project for more than ten years on this subject. ARF tracks TV, online, video and mobile advertising for 500 CPG brands (consumer packaged goods companies like Coca Cola etc.). Those ARF studies have been measuring return on ad spend (ROAS). According to their findings, the ROAS (return on advertising spend) is highest for magazine advertising, followed by display ads, cross media (combine several medium), TV, mobile and finally at the bottom of the list digital video. Therefore, magazines are number one in terms of ROAS.

In practical terms what this means is that for every $1.00 spent on magazine advertising, advertisers estimate that some $3.94 is achieved in sales. However, please remember the results from the McKinsey research which showed that only 33% of CMO's say they 'can prove the quantitative impact of marketing'. This fact brings into question any ROI or ROAS findings we might observe from the research.

Therefore, what we might conclude from this analysis on marketing ROI is that; marketing managers must begin to better understand the benefits of marketing channels used, and they must improve their data analysis capabilities (leverage data and measurement). Furthermore, marketers must make sure that their creative output is the best it can be, if they wish to drive sales in digital channels. Furthermore, marketers must begin to figure out how to benefit from digital channels, because that is where consumers are spending most of their time.

Return on Advertising Spend (ROAS)

3.94 = For every $1.00 spent on advertising,
$3.94 is created in incremental sales

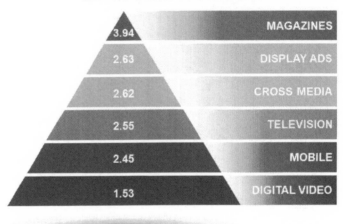

Source: The Advertising Research Foundation (2016)

Strategic Priorities

The discussion so far has focused mostly on tactical marketing issues (spend and ROI). However, the last hard data question every marketer should answer is;

What should be our strategic marketing priorities?

The Deloitte, Duke University, American Marketing Association CMO study discussed earlier, has also determined the strategic marketing priorities of companies today. The findings show that;

- 50% Market penetration strategies (% of respondents).
- 23% Product and service development.
- 16% Market development.
- 11% Diversification.

Based on these finding, we see that marketer's strategic priorities are focused mostly on penetrating existing markets, rather than growing markets. These findings are supported by a 2016 Salesforce.com survey of 4,000 full-time marketing leaders in North America, Europe, South America and Asia Pacific. Those marketing leaders said that their top three strategic marketing priorities were;

1. 35% Customer satisfaction (% of respondents).
2. 33% Revenue growth.
3. 24% Customer acquisition.

We can see from Salesforce.com findings that customer engagement is becoming increasingly important for marketers, and that increasing social media engagement has become a top priority. The Salesforce.com data estimates that digital will take a larger and larger share of marketing budgets. By 2021 marketers are expected to spend 75% of their total budget on digital marketing. However, to successfully implement these ambitious goals, marketers must determine how to best measure the impact of those investments.

Six Digital-age Marketing Rules

Despite all the hype these days surrounding digital, email campaigns, digital engagement and so on; the in-store experience still matter a great deal to marketers. What this means is that, marketers must also think beyond channels (TV, outdoor, and online etc.). They must do this because it is becoming increasingly important to create 'moments of enjoyment' their customers (experiential marketing). The company who can successfully create 'moments of joy' for their customer will in fact be winner in the digital age of marketing! Therefore, we could now conclude this marketing drill with Six Rules for marketers in the digital age;

1. Marketers must collect more data around customer touch points and purchases.
2. Marketers must learn to detect patterns in that data.
3. Marketers must begin to conduct more experiments, to help fine-tune their media choices.
4. Marketers must design a formula which can (with confidence) determine which touch-points to invest in, the synergy obtained from multiple consumer exposures to the same media over time, and how much to invest relatively to each area of spend.
5. Marketers determine the above formula can explains and predict outcomes (cause and effect).
6. Marketers must begin to accept complexity, especially due to the growth in Omni and Multi-channel marketing.

TASK: The Marketing Strategy Quiz

LINK: Marketing Strategy Quiz-McGraw Hill Inc.
https://goo.gl/R3osMk
Note: No registration is required for completing the quiz

SOURCES:

Moorman, C. (2016). The CMO Survey. Deloitte, Duke University and American Marketing Association

Winning in the Age of The Customer (2015). Forrester Research, Inc.

Digital Transformation: Re-imagine from the outside-in. Accenture Interactive

Expectations vs. Experience: The Good, the Bad, the Opportunity (2016). Forrester Research Inc.

Experiential Marketing Content Benchmarking Report (2016). Event Marketing Institute

Digital ad Spending Benchmarks by Industry (2016). eMarketer

DRILL 11: Digital Marketing

'Never be satisfied, always strive to improve' ~ Navy SEAL

1st Thing?

What is the first thing people do when they wake up in the morning, and what is the last thing they do, before they close their eyes and go to sleep? According to IDC research, for 80% of eighteen to forty-four-year old's, the first thing they do after waking up in the morning is to 'check their smartphone.' In fact, most people do that within fifteen minutes of waking, and over 60% of people reach for their smartphone immediately upon waking up. What do these facts mean for marketers today?

Mobile is King

Here is another bit of trivia which also demonstrates the important role that smartphones now play in everyone's lives. Just eight years ago, 80% of people's digital media time (daily time spent with digital media) was on a desktop or laptop computer, and only 12% was on a mobile device. Fast forward to the historical year of 2015, and the picture looked very different, you might even say historical. 2015 was historical because for the first time, mobile devices represented over 51% of adult daily digital media time. Therefore, the world became a mobile-first digital marketplace in 2015. In 2017 the global average time spent reading newspapers per day will be some fourteen minutes (-37% in just seven years), magazine readership has declined −23%, radio -15%, going to the movies -11%, watching television -8%, and even outdoor advertising has declined -3%. The important point to pay attention to here is that; the individual media activity areas which have been declining rapidly, still represent the major advertising channels used to promote products and services today.

Consumer Behavior

Despite the changes in behavior just discussed (decline in TV viewing habits etc.), the way people buy products remains rather traditional, and has not changed dramatically over time. For example, most consumers still shop for clothing, food, home goods and luxury items in a real store. Of course, we can see from the data that almost 20% of retail sales are online (and its growing fast) however, we should not forget that in-store shopping still represents over 70%+ of all retail sales. The important message here is that people still shop the same way but, the behavior of consumers is changing rapidly. Moreover, these behavioral changes are negatively impacting marketing channels which companies have relied on heavily in the past.

Experiential Marketing

In an earlier marketing drill, we talked about the need to improve customer experiences (experiential marketing). What the findings on shopping behavior tell us is that, despite all the hype on digital, in-store marketing must not be neglected. This message appears to be heard by marketers, as we can see from the breakdown in experiential marketing efforts being made by companies today;

- 45% In-store.
- 19% Social media.
- 14% Web-based.
- 11% Call centers.
- 6% Mobile-text.
- 5% email.

Digital Marketing

Based on this data, the story here is that; the future of marketing has almost everything to do with digital marketing. Therefore, in this Bootcamp we think it is wise to take a deep-dive into digital marketing. This is because, digital is the direction the market is moving in, and it is moving in that direction due to the changing behavior of people around the world. Furthermore, for most people, their digital devices have become one of the most important parts of their lives. However; are marketers aware of the behavior-shift which has been occurring, and how this shift is impacting the ways marketers engage with customers?

Online

According to the most recent Gartner Chief Marketing Officer (CMO) Study, the average company today allocates (spends) some 30% of their marketing budget in online marketing, and this percentage is expected to grow to 35% within the next three years. Of that budget, search engine marketing (SEO & SEM) will capture the largest share, and online display marketing (banner ads, online video, etc.) will take the second largest share. So where is social media in this mix? Well, social media investments are growing however, they represent only 15% of the total online spend by marketers. But here is an important point to keep in mind; mobile marketing has been grown so rapidly that it is now considered across all channels. Therefore, due to this spread, it has become increasingly difficult to even break down mobile spend figures.

Digital Media Spend

Despite mobile becoming the King of digital marketing channels! Before going any further in this analysis of marketing, it is important to understand how digital marketing spend looks in today's marketplace. Based on the most recent Forrester digital media research findings, the market spend is;

- 45% on Search (% of budget)
- 37% on Display
- 15% on Social
- 3% on email

This data is nice to know however, what is even more interesting to observe is that 'companies digital advertising spend has not responded to the changes in consumer behavior'. This fact can also be seen from the data on media ad spend by companies;

- 37% on TV (although viewing has declined -8% in five years).
- 36% on Digital (growing).
- 14% on Print (Reading has declined -35% in five years).
- 7% on Radio (Listening has declined -11% in five years).

Marketing Priorities

Based on the research data, by the year 2020 digital will represent 45% of media ad spend and TV 33%. Therefore, it is obvious that marketers have been slow in adjusting their strategies to the rapidly developing digital market-place. Furthermore, this seems to be true for both B2B and B2C companies. To emphasize this point, the most recent eMarketer research findings show that only 40% of marketers say their digital marketing techniques or methods are expanding, or they are already fully used in their marketing operations. However, those same marketers say that their future top marketing priorities for allocating or spending are;

- 40% Digital commerce (% of respondents).
- 40% Innovations in marketing.
- 37% Lead conversion.
- 36% Customer retention.

Mind the Gap

Based on the above data, one could ask the one-million-dollar marketing question;

Why is there such a big gap between people's digital behavior and money being spent by marketers on digital?

What the data is telling us is that one primary reason for the lag in spending vs. behavior; is due to the inability of marketers to justify the return on digital marketing investments (ROI). Therefore, marketers are having a hard time measuring the impact of their digital marketing efforts. Furthermore, it has been safer to continue concentrating on traditional marketing channels, as those marketers slowly try to figure out how to effectively manage digital channels. For the leading companies however, this learning is already being done through small digital marketing experiments.

ROI by Marketing Channel

Let's now quickly look at the research findings to see what we might discover about the digital marketing experiments which are giving the best ROI. Based on the percentage of marketing professionals who said that the ROI was excellent to good, we can see that social media-based marketing is the worst performer and social is followed by online display ads.

The above finding (social media-based marketing performance) is interesting. Especially if one considers how much time people currently spend on social media platforms. Next on the list of worst performers is mobile marketing, followed by affiliate marketing. By now you might be wondering; what are the best performing (ROI) digital marketing channels today? Well the research reveals this information and it seems that Content Marketing, SEO (search engine marketing), and email are currently the best performing digital media marketing channels today. Some 63% of marketers say that content marketing ROI is excellent to good, and 67% say that SEO ROI is excellent too good. However, the King of the digital marketing ROI mountain is (the highest level of ROI on marketing) email. Almost 70% (68% to be exact) of all marketers in the eMarketer research said that email had an excellent to good ROI. That was a surprise even for the Mini MBA Bootcamp leader!

ROI By Channel
Excellent to Good (% of respondents)

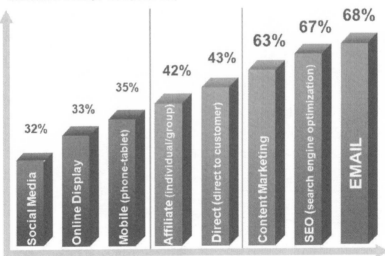

Source: eMarketer

By now we should all have a better appreciation of the challenges which marketers everywhere are facing. As customers engage more and more through digital, these challenges will only grow. Measuring ROI seems to be one of the major challenges as the shift in behavior occurs. However, marketers are also facing numerous other challenges. According to the recent SimpleMeasured report called 'State of Social Media Marketing'. The top three challenges faced by social media professionals in North America include;

1. Measuring ROI.
2. Creating systems to track the results of marketing efforts.
3. Understanding real performance across social channels.

Here is an important point to keep in mind when reviewing all this data. The data is only revealing the big picture on digital media challenges faced by marketers. Please remember though that, depending on a company's area of business (B2B, B2C), along with their unique product/service-offering, strategy and capabilities, this shopping list of challenges might look very different for each individual case. As a matter of fact, some of the less critical challenges might be very critical to the success of some businesses, despite what the macro-data reveals. Please keep this in mind when interpreting this data.

Social Media

We are now coming to the end of this discussion on digital marketing therefore; it makes sense to end our discussion with some data on social media. We should do this because, social was one, if not, the worst performing marketing ROI channel. The research data can help us to understand which social media channels are most effective today (ROI). Please keep in mind that social media was one of the most challenging marketing channels and is performing very badly on ROI.

Based on the most recent data available, the social media platform that produces the best ROI is Facebook, (96% of marketers say that Facebook is best). However, remember that every social media channel serves a different purpose. Therefore, it is important for a company to determine first; which social media channel serves their purposes best (strategy), and for those a company's ROI performance might in fact be better than the average. Furthermore, one must remember that over 80% of people's social media access is on a mobile device. Therefore, it is no surprise that in the most recent AdMedia Partners research report marketing executives say the most important digital growth area in the future is mobile (followed by social, video, content, programmatic, search and finally display advertising).

DRILL 11: Summary

1. The world has become a mobile-first digital marketplace however, marketers continue to invest mostly in traditional media channels. Marketers need to determine how to measure and improve ROI in digital media channels.
2. Online marketing continues to grow, and mobile will grow even faster. Therefore; innovative marketing approaches are needed, along with improved performance measurement and analysis tools.
3. Despite the revolution occurring in digital, marketers should not neglect their existing customers. Furthermore, the importance of in-store marketing is growing. Effective in-store marketing requires companies to create lasting experiences (experiential marketing) during those moments when people are shopping. This is important because in-store marketing is still one of the most promising marketing channels.

TASK: Marketing Quiz

LINK: Online Marketing Quiz-McGraw Hill
https://goo.gl/2if6fQ
Note: No registration is required for the quiz

SOURCES:

Digital Transformation: Re-imagine from the outside-in. Accenture Interactive

Digital ad Spending Benchmarks by Industry (2016). eMarketer

Meeker, M. (2016). Internet Trends Report. KPCB

Dawson, A., Hirt, M., & Scanlan, J. (2016). The Economic Essential of Digital Strategy. McKinsey Quarterly

The 2016 State of Social Marketing Report (2016). Simply Measured

Wurmser, Y. (2016). Performance Marketing. eMarketer

Genovese, Y. Sorofman, J., & Virzi, A.M. (2016). Gartner CMO Spend Survey 2015-2016. Gartner Inc.

DRILL 12: TECHNOLOGY

'People do not follow robots' ~ Navy SEAL

According to Vinnie Mirchandani who wrote the popular book; The New Technology Elite, every business is now a technology business. Mirchandani says that; tech-savvy companies, whether they sell insurance or airplanes, are now becoming tech vendors, and that in the future this will become true for most companies. What will that mean for managers? If this becomes the reality, one of the major challenges in being a tech company is that things change very fast and because of that, every tech company must learn to change fast!

DIGITALIZATION SKILLS

Accenture research found that companies must learn five critical skills to effectively adopt new technologies into their businesses and be able to change fast. Those five critical skills are;

1. Developing new and more powerful information analysis and intelligence-range capabilities.
2. Defining business processes that support continuous collaboration between employees, suppliers, agents and customers.
3. Integrating digital technology into all functions that support efficiency.
4. Re-imagining the traditional customer-management model, and moving away from transactions, to more individual customer relationships.
5. Building and using systems that allow for real-time decision making.

Lego: The Apple Corp. Of Toys

To understand better the five Accenture technology adoption skills, let's discuss another Mini Case. By using a Mini-Case we can better understand the five technology-adoption skills discovered by Accenture. This Mini Case will be on the Lego Toy Company. For our purposes, we could call Lego the 'Apple Corporation of Toys'.

Lego produce 3,000 unique Lego bricks, in more than 50 color options. Since the Apple Corp. of Toys was established in 1932, more than 760 billion Lego bricks (elements) have been manufactured. This means that on average every person on this earth owns over 100 Lego bricks. The great success of Lego is partially due to the realization of management that 'Lego needed to become modern'. Lego started the process of modernization by first studying how kids around the world play (*information analysis capability*). Lego even appointed a Lego Professor of Learning Research in their company (*information intelligence capability*).

When Lego first began their modernization program and studying how kids play (*information analysis capability*), what they discovered was that kids don't see a difference between digital playing and snapping together Lego bricks. Because of that discovery, Lego began to combine their bricks with software tools which kids could run on their phones or computers (*integrating digital technology into the business*). What emerged from this experiment was the Lego 'digital play experience'. Now that is interesting however, today two-thirds of Lego revenues (turnover) is from new products that did not even exist a year ago.

The digital play experience at Lego has also meant that Lego introduced 'digital only' experiences (Fusion Portal Racers). The Fusion game, is a PC game that responds to body movements, as if one were inside the game (*developing more individual customer relationships*). However, the digital awakening at Lego can be best seen at the enterprise-level. Lego are exploring more than ten different digital priorities, and only two of those priorities are directly related to toy products. Three of the ten digitalization priorities are built around marketing, and five (50% of their digitalization program) is at the enterprise level (*integrating digital technology into all functions to become more efficient*), which covers the complete corporation.

Digitalization @LEGO

ENTERPRISE	MARKETING	PRODUCT
Enterprise IT platform	Omni-channel marketing	Combine physical and Digital
Design engagement platform	Digital engagement with LEGO community	Crowd-source innovation (community platforms)
Responsive IT Organization	Globalize digital assets (intellectual property)	
Appoint digital officers		
Digital workforce and environment		

Source: Sawey,. O.A (University of Southern California (2015)

Although Lego have been working very hard to rapidly develop their digital capability, group management has still never lost sight of the fact that their long-term focus is on the core business. That core business is the Lego bricks. The important point here is that despite the allure of digitalization, every company must remember to understand and value their core business, even if that business is a small color brick. Furthermore, efforts must be made in every business to develop the level of digitalization and that effort should be connected to and supporting the core business. A company's core business can always change but until it does all efforts, including digitalization, must support the core business. For Lego, that core business is a tiny little brick which helps kids to learn. That little Lego brick has helped create $5 billion Toy Empire. However, the digitalization of Lego (the Apple of Toys) does raise an interesting question; is Lego Unique in doing this?

Digitalization Strategy

According to a most recent Forrester report 'On Digitalization Efforts by Companies'. Only 27% of businesses today have a logical digitalization strategy (have defined how they will create customer value as a digital business). This means than 70%+ of companies don't have a digitalization strategy. In this Mini MBA drill, we will focus-in on digitalization of businesses. We will do this because; digitalization will have a big impact on every business, and every manager must understand the impact of this trend.

The Forrester research findings referred to above (27% of businesses today have a digitalization strategy), could also be interpreted to mean that; digital transformation is not a strategic priority for most companies today. However, answer to that interpretation is NO! In fact, digitalization today is a top priority for most companies, and this can be seen from the findings of many research reports (Gartner, IDC, Forrester etc.). Furthermore, some studies have come up with predictions on the impact of digitalization in companies. Those predictions are very interesting for our purposes of understand the changing business landscape;

- 35% of all Information Technology (IT) resources in companies (by 2018), will be spent to support the creation of new digital revenue streams (earnings a business makes from all the methods).
- 50% of IT budgets will be tied to digital transformation actions (by 2020).

e-Commerce

This digitalization rush-hour is occurring because for many businesses, digital thinking and technology is a matter of survival. Therefore, the impact of digitalization on businesses has quickly evolved from; why to how a company can implement and operationalize a digital strategy? Part of the digitalization rush hour must be to do with the rapid growth of online buying (e-commerce). Today, about $1.5 trillion is spent online, and that number is expected to grow to $2.5 trillion by the year 2018. That means the e-commerce marketplace is growing at a compounded growth rate of over +12% annually. Not bad, especially for a business that is rapidly going online. Therefore, the potential is quite large when comparing the growth of e-commerce sales vs total retail sales. According to Nielson, China's online retail sales already represent 12% or more of total retail sales (8% in USA). However, despite the small overall percentages, e-commerce annual growth rates are from +30% to +50%. Furthermore, China is already the largest e-commerce market in the world, with North America representing the second largest market (33%).

International e-Commerce

Please remember that e-commerce sales in regions of the world other that North America and Europe are growing rapidly (India and Brazil etc.). To emphasize the importance of those markets, mobile e-commerce (which has a small overall share), is witnessing very rapid growth rates in India. Mobile e-commerce already represents more than 50% of all online retail sales in that country. That is an impressive statistic which everyone interested in mobile-commerce should keep an eye on.

There are other trends which are driving the digitalization revolution. For example, the typical information technology department in a company will spend up to 30% of their total budget on risk, security and compliance by 2018 (all linked to online business activities). Furthermore, companies will allocate 10%+ of their information technology staff to those activities. In addition, by 2018, at least 20% of all workers will use automated assistance technologies to help them make decisions. More than three million workers worldwide are expected to be already supervised by a Robo-Boss. Robo-Boss is an algorithm or smart-machine that monitors worker accomplishments and evaluates performance through measurements which are directly tied to output and customer evaluations.

Digital Marketing

To get a more concrete understanding of how technology is impacting businesses, let's return for a moment to the subject of an earlier Mini MBA drill on marketing. During that drill we agreed that it is essential to reflect on how technology is impacting marketing. As we learned in that session, marketing is increasingly becoming more technology-oriented. There is even a buzz-word for this trend called MarTech (Mar = marketing, and Tech = technology). To emphasize the importance of the MarTech trend, according to Gartner research technology investments by marketers will soon be greater than what Information Technology departments currently invest within companies. Furthermore, the most important technology investment for marketers will be, in order of priority:

1. Social Marketing
2. Digital Commerce
3. Analytics

High performing companies in the Gartner research, were found to be four to ten times more likely to be already using these technologies. Furthermore, there are many emerging technologies which high performance companies are already experimenting with, such as;

- Proximity Marketing: Localized wireless distribution of advertising content associated with a physical place.
- Internet of Things: Network connectivity between everyday objects which allows them to send and receive data.
- Podcasting: Digital media files a user can set up or automatically download via the web.
- Wearables: Electronics that can be worn on the body, either as an accessory or as part of material used in clothing.
- Artificial Intelligence (AI).

The million-dollar technology question for many companies today is;

What should be our digitalization strategy?

To help answer that question, one must keep in mind that; every company needs to consider how likely it might be that the new technologies will disrupt their current markets and businesses? By disruption, we mean an innovation that creates a new market and value network, which eventually disrupts existing markets and value networks. This often occurs because the disruptive technologies displace or replace existing company's products, alliances or networks. Therefore, it is vital for companies to understand (especially before it happens) if there are technologies out there which might disrupt their market, and why this might happen?

Digital Disruption

There are two primary reasons why digital disruption might happen to a business. The first of those reasons is that digitalization creates new markets. This occurs when new suppliers identify cheaper and easier ways of doing things (which meet un-met demand in the marketplace). On this point, it is important to realize that most companies today are primarily focused on serving existing customers, who are most attractive for their business. This often means that a large share of the potential market (with emphasis on the word potential) is currently not being served. The gap between served and un-served markets often represents a great opportunity for companies who are disrupting marketplaces.

The second and more dangerous disruption which can occur is when disruptors improve products or services through technology. For example, a disruptive competitor might virtualize the supply of a product (Amazon) or they might automate and existing manual process (Uber), or they might do more of the work for customers because they offer better connectivity and information (Google in education). There are many other examples of these digitalization risks. McKinsey research has highlighted some of the danger signals which might suggest that a business is ripe for disruption. Those danger signs include;

- Better information or social media could greatly improve the product or service.
- A physical product (light bulb or thermostat) is not yet 'connected' to other devices or systems.
- There's a gap between the point when customers purchase a product or service, and the time they receive it.
- Customers still must physically go and get a product or service (groceries are a great example of this).

Digitalization Forces and Actions

ACTIONS	FORCES		
	DEMAND	SUPPLY	DEMAND & SUPPLY
MODERATE ❑ Make products easier & faster ❑ Make products cheaper ❑ Tailor/Personalize products ❑ Unbundle product features ❑ ID new supply sources ❑ Create smaller supply moments	UNDISTORTED DEMAND	UNCONSTRAINED SUPPLY	NEW MARKETS
EXTREME ❑ Enrich products with information ❑ Do more work for customers ❑ Enhance customer relations ❑ Form network of companies ❑ Automation/Virtualization	NEW VALUE PROPOSITIONS	HYPER-SCALE PLATFORMS	NEW BUSINESS SYSTEMS

Source: McKinsey & Company

Case: Amazon Dash Button

One very exciting example of this digitalization trend is the Amazon Dash Button. The Dash Button is a Wi-Fi connected device that re-orders your favorite product with the press of a button through your Amazon app.

The way the Dash Button works is that you simply set it up, close to where the product you wish to re-order is kept (for example your washing detergent in the closet). When you notice that you are running out of that product, you push the Dash Button, and that product is automatically reordered for you on Amazon. You don't need to worry about someone else pushing the button just after you have, because Dash Button responds only to your first press, until your order is delivered; regardless of how many times Dash Button is pressed.

Furthermore, you receive an order notification (if enabled) for every order placed. This allows you to cancel an order before it ships. The Dash Button is a great example of a case where customers no longer must physically go and get a product or service.

Finally, the dangers of disruption (according to McKinsey) can increase because other companies might have identified new ways to charge customers for their products or services. In other words, they have figured out a way to get someone else to pay for the cost of their doing business. A great example here is: YouTube, Google, Facebook and other online services providers. Who is paying for those services?

Every business must learn to recognize and consider what actions are needed to manage the potential digital disruption of their business. However, those actions will always depend on the level of threat each company faces (or recognizes). However, be aware that according to the research, most of companies are unprepared for the move to digital business models (McKinsey research). This move includes online products, sales and services, which will 'begin to dominate their revenue potential of companies within the next five years'.

McKinsey research shows that more than four out of five companies (84%) do not have the necessary skills and talent to execute the required digital transformation. Therefore, although disruption will be common in the future, most companies are not prepared, and do not have the required skills or strategies to deal with this looming threat! Based on the content of this session everyone should realize that every company must be prepared for the digital era of business!

DRILL 12: Summary

1. Every business is already, or is becoming, a technology business. This will have a big impact on how businesses operate in the future.
2. 27% of companies have a logical digital strategy which clearly sets out how they will create customer value as a digital business.
3. Every company should be monitoring and aware of the danger signals which might indicate that their business is ripe for digital disruption.

TASK: View Raising Digital Quotient (McKinsey)

In a recent McKinsey research study, over 200 companies that are digital winners had one common thread; A high Digital Quotient (DQ).

McKinsey Video (2:00 min. video)
https://goo.gl/hiR3Gt
Note: The video links bring you to the Dr. G.L. Danford video library.

SOURCES:

Mirchandani, V. (2012). The Technology Elite

The Digital Business Transformation Playbook (2016). Forrester Research Inc.

The Organizational Health Index. McKinsey & Co.

Hopkins, B., Doty, C., & Belissent, J. (2015). Predications 2016. The Path from Data to Action for Marketers. Forrester Research

Laney, D. et. al. Predicts 2016: Information Strategy (2015). Gartner

Omar, E.S., Kraemmergaard, P., Amsinck, H., & Vinther, A.L. (2015). Building the Foundations and Enterprise Capabilities for Digital Leadership. Society for Information Management

Worldwide Digital Transformation Predictions (2015). IDC

DRILL 13: SUSTAINABILITY

'We are part of something greater than ourselves' ~ Navy SEAL

Companies are always trying to identify ways to be different from their competition. Companies are also always trying to find ways to add-value for their customers. Therefore, in this Mini MBA drill we will discuss a quite exciting idea. This is exciting because, this idea is a way for companies to achieve two goals (differentiation and added-value). Furthermore, these ideas have been neglected by many companies. The way to simultaneously differentiate and add-value way is by deploying a sustainability strategy. But what is a sustainability strategy? Please think about that for a moment before continuing to read!

Sustainability Strategy

A good definition of a sustainability strategy might be as follows:

> *'A business that has a minimal negative impact on the global, local, community, society, and economic environment. Furthermore, that business strives to meet the Triple Bottom Line'.*

The Triple Bottom Line, often called TBL, is an accounting framework that is made up of three components: social, environmental (ecological), and financial. The bottom line refers to either profit or loss, because those are the items which are usually recorded at the very bottom line on a statement of revenue and expenses. That's why it is called the bottom line.

Now here's another important question to consider;

What % of companies has a sustainability strategy; 0%, 25%, 75%, 100%?

Based on research by the Massachusetts Institute of Technology (MIT), and the Boston Consulting Group (BCG), 40% of companies today have a sustainability strategy, and another 20% have tried but found it extremely difficult. And now here is the alarming number, 40% of companies don't have one, or don't even know if they have one. Therefore, this Mini MBA drill we will focus-in on describing the benefits of having a sustainability strategy, along with how a manager can measure those benefits. To achieve these objectives, we will present some of the most recent research findings on this most important topic.

Based on research by MIT and BCG, it seems that most companies are still struggling with sustainability. In concrete business terms what this means is that; companies are still trying to figure out how to build sustainability into their business model, their budgeting, and their supply chain practices, therefore, sustainability is not an easy goal to achieve. However, on the bright side, one could say that because of this struggle, there still exists in most businesses a lot of potential to increase value creation by having a sustainability strategy. The challenge however is; any company who wants to become a sustainability leader must first answer some very hard questions, including;

1. What are the best Key Performance Indicators (KPI's) for sustainability?
2. What is the right organizational structure for a sustainable business strategy?
3. How does a company get top management committed to a sustainability strategy?

Business Case

According to MIT and BCG research, the best way to answer those questions is by first establishing a strong business case for sustainability throughout the organization. However, the need to establish a strong business case raises the question; what is the business case for sustainability?

Often, when managers think about sustainability in their company, they think mostly about the company's reputation. In other words, managers think that being sustainable 'is good for publicity'. However, the research by MIT and BCG highlights an important point regarding this matter. What they found in their research was that for a company to become a sustainability leader (in a real business value sense), requires that the company must move beyond just thinking about reputation and publicity. So why should a company move beyond thinking about sustainability as just reputation and publicity? Well, according to the research this is necessary because companies who are most successful with their sustainability efforts have been the ones who created value in multiple areas of their business through their sustainability efforts. The important point to remember here is that; the value a company creates from a sustainability program can have a bigger impact on more than just a company's reputation.

Value Creation

To illustrate the above point on value creation, that value which is created can include; increased growth, lower levels of risk, and a positive impact for return on capital. Unfortunately, according to MIT and BCG, few companies are realizing these potential benefits of in their sustainability strategy. This fact raises an important question for us in the Mini MBA and that is; why are companies not realizing the value-added benefits from sustainability, and what actions can be taken to make a strong business case for sustainability? One reason companies have not succeeded in establishing a successful sustainability strategy is that when most companies are considering a sustainability strategy, they don't remember that different industries and even different companies within the same industry, can benefit from different sustainability levers. By levers we mean those actions which will have the greatest impact on the sustainability efforts made. In other words, most companies don't remember that sustainability levers can create significant value however, those levers will be different in every business. What this means is that there is no one-size-fits-all solution to an effective sustainability strategy. This simple fact is one of the most important lessons to learn in this Mini

MBA drill because, there isn't only one way to create value from a sustainability program.

It's critical for each company to design a sustainability strategy which is unique for that company. Now that may sound too simple of a solution for such a complex problem however, this finding is supported by the research and the success of leading sustainability company cases. When formulating a unique sustainability strategy, a company should identify where the biggest opportunities for value creation might exist. In addition to this important point, each company must also identify sustainability-related risks which are unique for their business activities. Furthermore, it is essential to identifying the barriers which exist within the organization that will prevent them from achieving success. According to MIT and McKinsey, then and only then can a company implement a successful sustainability strategy!

What is the concrete business case for having a sustainability strategy, and what can we learn from the success cases on this matter? Well we have some interesting findings on these issues, based on the sustainability research findings of McKinsey. Those research findings are surprising because the benefits of having an effective sustainability program can be seen in some unexpected business activities. For sustainability leaders, the research shows that the greatest benefits have been;

- More effectively reaching new customers (the sustainability effort resulted in companies expanding their existing customer base).
- Becoming more effective in research and development (R&D) by identifying novel solutions and testing those solutions in the marketplace.

However, the sad news from the research findings is that only 30% of all other companies studied were taking sustainability-related actions to reach new customers or to improve their R&D. What this means is that most companies today are still not realizing two of the most important business-case benefits from having a sustainability strategy.

What is that all about? Are companies blind to the opportunities or do they feel that an effective sustainability strategy requires too much effort? What do you think?

Sustainability Value Creation

Value Levers	VALUE CREATION	VALUE CREATION	VALUE CREATION	Metrics
GROWTH	**PORTFOLIO** Guides Investment decisions	**INNOVATION** Develop products, technologies (meet customer R&D needs)	**MARKETS** Identifies market segments and geographical opportunities	
RETURN ON CAPITAL	**MARKETING** Increase sales, premium pricing (green) or market share	**VALUE CHAIN** Reduce costs, improve value proposition (environmental)	**OPERATIONS** Reduce operating costs (improved Resource management/costs	
RISK MANAGEMENT	**OPERATIONAL** Manage risks (resource scarcity, climate change...	**REPUTATION** Reduce reputation risks, get credit for actions (stakeholder management)	**REGULATION** Capture opportunities from regulations & mitigate risks	

Good ---------------------------> Poor

Sustainability Actions

The McKinsey research findings can help explain why companies are not realizing the benefits of having a sustainability strategy. McKinsey carrier out research on how the leading companies begin their sustainability program, along with identifying the best areas to focus ones' efforts on first, to extract the maximum business- value from those efforts. What they learned from that research is first; most of the leading companies began their sustainability initiatives by focusing-in on reducing resource consumption. As an example of this, 97% of the leading companies explored ways to increase energy efficiency in their business processes. In addition to this, 91% looked at ways to reduce waste in their processes, and a further 85% explored how they could save water in their day-to-day operations. Based on this finding, we can see that leading companies have focused their first sustainability efforts on areas that have had a direct impact on their day to day business operational costs.

In addition to focusing-in on costs, the leading companies also paid attention to business risks and how sustainability might help reduce or mitigate those risks. 90% of the leading companies identified a specific event or risk which could negatively impact their business, and more importantly, their sustainability actions could help reduce those risks. Some of those risks included; the risk of growing consumer pressure on their business, and the risk of soaring commodity prices (impact on costs).

The most important to remember on this point is that; by first identifying significant risks for the business, the leading companies could then increase the commitment for sustainability within their companies. What this means is that by identifying a major risk for their business, management and leadership in those companies then began to pay more attention to, and to take more seriously, the benefits sustainability efforts might have for their business. Because of this, sustainability became more visible on the leadership radar. One additional insight gained from the research on the success of sustainability leaders was that; 44% of the leading companies said that growth opportunities were the primary reason for starting their sustainability program. Therefore, one could say that sustainability is good for business!

Risks

The research findings also revealed a major risk for any sustainability effort. The leading companies quickly recognized that no sustainability initiative can create lasting value if it is poorly managed. What this warning means is that; how a company executes and implements their sustainability initiatives is critical for success to occur. This warning raises one of the most important challenges regarding the creation of a successful sustainability strategy and that challenge is; how can a company define and individualized a sustainability strategy for their unique business context? What do you think is the answer to that question?

Focus

The McKinsey research identified four best practices which can help to; individualized a sustainability strategy for a unique business context. First the company must identify one focus area that has the best fit with their corporate strategy and their entire value chain (activities from inputs, through processing and final outputs in a company). Unfortunately, this focus can only be achieved by completing a thorough internal analysis of the business, along with having supplier, customer, and regulator discussions. However, this homework can pay off if the company identifies one significant impact opportunity.

Measurable Goals

Second, a company must set clear and measurable long-term sustainability goals (for a period of five years or more). In addition to setting those goals, it is also essential to communicate the goals internally and externally. Effective communication is necessary because making public those quantifiable goals can help motivate the whole organization. Furthermore, it will incentivize leaders in the organization to allocate the necessary resources, for those goals to be achieved. In addition to this, effective communication helps to target the right individuals in the organization who will eventually become accountable for those goals.

Therefore, every company should remember that goals are great, but communication of goals is just as important. This is because the communication of goals also helps create a sense of urgency in the organization. Setting goals might seem to be an obvious thing to do however, 33% of companies in the research said that they had not defined Key Performance Indicators (KPI's) for sustainability. Because they did not set goals, people in their organization were not being held accountable for their actions. Therefore, if you remember anything from this

Bootcamp drill, please remember that without accountability, very little is going to happen!

Cost/Benefit Analysis

Third, a cost-benefit analysis of the goals must be completed, and companies must communicate widely the findings of that analysis. Unfortunately, in the case of sustainability, the problem with making a cost benefit analysis is that the savings and profits resulting from sustainability initiatives are often widely spread across an organization. What this means is that a great deal of effort must go into quantify the financial impact. However, quantify the impact is critical to remember because only 20% of companies in the McKinsey research could report and communicate the financial benefits of their sustainability efforts. However, there is a solution to this problem. For sustainability leaders, that solution involved selecting one individual executive who will be the 'owner' of each sustainability target. Those executives will continually track the costs and benefits of the sustainability actions.

Tracking costs and benefits allows the sustainability 'owners' to measure the indirect effects (improved corporate reputation and increased customer loyalty etc.). Tracking is also important because often, sustainability benefits only pay off in the longer run, and that is why 37% percent of companies in the McKinsey research said that having only a focus on short-term earnings is often the reason for poor results. Furthermore, having a short-term perspective on sustainability is a big mistake because sustainability programs will often only pay off in the longer-term.

Creating Incentives

Fourth, the number one reason companies gave for not being able to capture the full value of sustainability efforts was that they had not clearly defined the incentives. The research shows that only 8% of companies included sustainability measures when calculating performance-based compensation for their executives. Furthermore, only 14% of companies rewarded suppliers for good sustainability performance. Therefore, incentives and rewards are critical for success to occur in any sustainability effort. Without incentives being put in place, people in the organization quickly return to the normal behavior which has rewarded them in the past.

By now you are probably getting overwhelmed by all this data on sustainability. However, please remember that in business; you cannot manage what you cannot measure. Therefore, to fully understand how your company can be successful with their sustainability program, it is necessary that we cover just a few more critical data points. After that we will draw some conclusions on this strategically important subject.

Benefits of Sustainability

Now it's about time that we considered what are the concrete benefits of having a clearly defined and measurable sustainability program? Well, the benefits can be seen in operational efficiency and operating costs. 33% of companies in the McKinsey research said their sustainability programs improved operational efficiency and lowered their costs. In addition, 32% said that sustainability enhanced or improved their corporate reputation, and 31% said that the sustainability efforts were aligned with the company's business goals, mission, and values. In other words, sustainability was supporting the strategy of the entire company, which is very important for any activities carried out in a company. 27% said that sustainability efforts created new growth opportunities for the company. However, this made me wonder (and might make you wonder), what do these findings mean for the 70%+ of other companies who did not see these benefits?

Best Practices

In business we talk a lot about best practices and what we can learn from others. So, let's now go briefly through the best sustainability practices of the leading companies, and see what we might learn from those practices. Fortunately for us, there are many lessons to be learned.

- **Lesson 1**: Sustainability leaders have shifted from viewing sustainability as a form of reputation management, towards viewing it as one way to achieve operational improvements and create new growth opportunities. What this means is that the leading sustainability companies have become more business-like with regards to their sustainability agenda.

- **Lesson 2**: Sustainability leaders have identified and defined sustainability Key Performance Indicators (KPI's) and created the proper organizational structures for achieving those KPI's.

- **Lesson 3**: Sustainability leaders have actively engaged the company's leadership in the sustainability agenda. 94% of the leading sustainability companies had integrated sustainability into the strategic planning process (only 53% of all other companies did this).

- **Lesson 4**: Sustainability leaders have aligned sustainability with their strategy. 59% of the leader companies had aligned sustainability with their corporate goals, mission, and values (only 28 percent of all other companies did this).

- **Lesson 5**: Sustainability leaders use sustainability as a recruiting/employee retaining tool: 53% of sustainability leaders had promoted their sustainability efforts as one way to attract new employees, and to help keep existing employees.

- **Lesson 6**: Sustainability leaders achieved value-creation. Regarding value creation. 48% percent of the leading sustainability companies said that sustainability has contributed to short-term value creation.

- **Lesson 7**: Sustainability leaders improved their competitive standing. 43% percent of the leader companies said that they have improved their competitive position on the market (24% percent for others).

- **Lesson 8**: Only 9% of the leading companies said that their sustainability program was focused on responding to regulatory requirements and corporate reputation (25 percent of all other companies gave this reason).

It might feel like we have been focusing far too much on the hard data surrounding sustainability. However, please remember that without evidence to support sustainability, you are unlikely to get the necessary support from everyone in the organization. Therefore, gathering and presenting the hard facts is essential for any sustainability effort to succeed. Moreover, that hard data helps to sell the sustainability agenda within the organization. However, we must all remember that despite all this hard data, sustainability can and should mean different things for different companies.

Sustainability efforts are heavily influenced by the industry a company is active in. As an example of this, the McKinsey research findings varied a lot for companies who are active in business-to-consumer (B2C) or business-to-business (B2B). For example; 23% of B2B and 15% of B2C companies said sustainability programs positively impacted their reputation and increased shareholder value. This important finding reminds us of how important the individual context is for each individual company, and why it is essential for companies to tailor their sustainability strategy to their unique business context.

DRILL 13: Summary

1. Few companies (37%) have a sustainability strategy that can be justified at the "bottom line".

2. The three areas where the most impact can be achieved from a sustainability strategy are;
   a. Growth.
   b. Return on capital (ROC).
   c. Better risk management.

   Growth occurs because companies can reach new markets & customers. Return on capital (ROC) occurs because sustainable products and services can often command higher prices and improve market share. Lowering of risks occurs because of the impact from better reputation management.

3. Every company must first identify (for their unique business context) just one or two sustainability actions which have the best fit with their corporate strategy and that will have the greatest impact on their business performance. Those must then be precisely defined and measured with the right KPI's, as the company rolls-out their sustainability program and starts to benefit from an effectively and efficiently executed sustainability strategy.

TASK: Sustainability Assessment

The free tool (Pure Strategies) is a web-based survey with 12 short questions that takes less than ten minutes to complete. Your answers are compared to best practices identified from Pure Strategies' market research and a report is immediately provided that includes customized recommendations for improvement.

LINK: Product Sustainability Assessment
https://goo.gl/1GSpjw
Note: Registration required for free assessment.

TASK: The Green Quiz

National Geographic and WWF offer many online quizzes which test an individual's green knowhow, and how to shrink ones' environmental footprint! Sustainability begins at a personal level therefore, understanding your sustainability habits will help you to enlighten others.

LINK: National Geographic Green Quiz Page
https://goo.gl/WE0uUd

LINK: WWF Footprint Calculator
https://goo.gl/Uc3YPL
Note: No registrations required for quiz.

SOURCES:

Berg, A., Schlag, N., & Matuchtey, M. (2015). Getting the Most Out of Your Sustainability Program. McKinsey and Co.

Unruh, G. et al. (2016). Investing for a Sustainable Future. MIT Sloan Management Review

Kiron, D. et al. (2013). Sustainability's Next Frontier. MIT Sloan Management Review

Clark, G., Feiner, A., & Viehs, M. (2015). From the Stockholder to the Stakeholder. University of Oxford and Arabesque Partners

DRILL 14: OPERATIONS

'Freedom to operate and maneuver through disciplined procedures' ~ Navy
SEAL

Let's begin this Mini MBA drill on operations with two simple metaphors.
A metaphor is a word, phrase or even an image that can be used to make
a comparison between two things. So here are our two Bootcamp
metaphors for operations management.

Metaphors for Operations

WATERFALL: Imagine a waterfall. There's no question where this waterfall
is going, it's going down, and the water is taking you and everyone else
where you are going, and that one direction is down. At first, that
waterfall might be fun and exciting but, what if half way down the
waterfall you decide that you want to go back up to the top or maybe you
want to take a sudden turn to the left or the right? Unfortunately,
waterfalls are not designed for change. Waterfalls are not about to
change, and because of this, everything is going in one direction...down.

LAKE: Now image a peaceful lake. Your goal is to get to another place on
the lake, but that other place has not been precisely defined. However,
you know that the other place you seek should be somewhere better than
where you are now. In other words, it should be a place where the
opportunities are greater. Based on teamwork and the best information
available, you can make better decisions, even at the last minute as you
explore the lake. As you travel on the lake and explore the distant areas,
you eventually find a place that everyone agrees looks nice. You have
arrived at a new shore, with presents opportunities and new possibilities
for everyone.

The waterfall metaphor we imagined in this story represents the
traditional form of operational thinking. The lake metaphor, on the other
hand, represents a more agile way of thinking. So now the question for

you is; would you like your company's operations to look more like the waterfall or like a lake?

In most businesses, operations management is responsible for creating the highest level of efficiency (waterfall) for the organization. To achieve this goal, operations management teams attempt to balance costs with revenue, in the hope of achieving the highest possible net operating profit for the company. Therefore, the efficiency indicator often watched is EBIT (EBIT = revenue less expenses).

For the purposes of this Mini MBA Drill, operations management includes;

- Supply chain.
- Logistics.
- Production.
- Quality.
- Distribution of goods and services.

Stability & Change

Based on the above discussion, one can recognize that operations management is responsible for a very diverse set of activities. However, one major challenge for operations managers is to effectively manage stability and change at the same time. To do this successfully, requires both effectiveness and efficiency. Both are necessary because many businesses today operate under both stable and dynamically changing conditions. Under stable conditions, companies are resilient, reliable, and efficient, and management's role is to fine tune that efficiency and reliability. However, under dynamic conditions, the company must be fast, nimble, adaptive, agile and able to change as necessary.

These stable and dynamic conditions are often opposing one another, and because of this, they cause tension in the organization. To effectively deal with that tension, managers should design; structures, governance arrangements and processes that have both a relatively unchanging set of core components (back bore). However, at the same time, managers must create looser and more dynamic structures which are able to adapt quickly to new challenges and opportunities as they arise.

The capabilities needed to achieve the required balancing act (stable vs. dynamic) are very different and challenging. They are challenging because most efficient operations (pay attention to the word efficient) are highly tuned to carry out very specific activities. The fact that they are highly tuned often makes them inflexible to change. However, as we all know by now, the business environment for most companies today is experiencing continuous, if not discontinuous change on a regular basis. To survive and prosper in the future, company operations must be able to deal with both stable conditions that can be optimized for efficiency, along with much more uncertain conditions. During those uncertain conditions, the organization must be able to adapt quickly and change as necessary.

Therefore, managing stability and change is one of the most important and challenging tasks for operations management. To understand this challenge better, let's now discuss an operations MINI-CASE on the Lego Group.

Case: Lego Operations

Ole Kirk Christiansen was the founder of Lego (Lego are still a family-controlled company). Ole Kirk was a carpenter in Denmark, who started making wooden toys in 1932. The company name Lego means to 'play well' in the Danish language. That small wooden toy company, founded by Ole Kirk, today has a turnover of almost $5.5 billion and outperforms all other toy industry competitors. Lego has an operating profit of 34%, which is a good (25% is generally considered to be exceptionally good). Apple Corp. has a 30% operating profit.

The Lego story has not always been a good one. In 2004 business was not positive or stable for Lego, and they made the biggest loss in the company's history (-€260m, or -$300m). Furthermore, Lego sales decreased by more than -30% in that year (-35% in the USA). Now you might be wondering; why was Lego doing so badly in 2004? That is a very good question to ask! However, the answer to that question is not so simple because, management at Lego recognized that there were multiple reasons for the company's bad performance. Just a few of those reasons for bad performance included:

- Three quarters of Lego sales were from non-electronic products, and the video game market was growing very fast. Due to the growth of electronic game sales, management considered; should they expand further into electronic toys?
- Lego may have too many operational areas (toys, parks, retail stores, etc.). Because of this, operations at Lego had become far too complex. The growing diversity of operations raised a challenging question for Lego management; should they rationalize or reduce the number of activities, and if so, which ones?
- The Lego supply chain was outdated and did not meet the needs of the current market conditions. Therefore, management had to consider if they should focus on over-hauling the supply chain?

Because of the many different reasons for bad performance in the group, Lego management decided to select one issue to focus on first. They did this because they understood that fixing one critical thing, is much easier that fixing three or more problems at the same time. However, despite the many challenges just listed, the Lego group was a very innovative company. Lego were considered innovative because they had already started introducing video games (recognized and responded to signals from the market). Furthermore, their Lego retail store expansion was a growing business. However, these innovative efforts were the source of many of the problems Lego faced. This was because, the expansion of activities at Lego were in fact dramatically increasing the complexity of their business. Therefore, complexity had become one of the greatest enemies for the company.

Lego management in 2004 came to the realization that they had to decide on one critical area to focus their recovery efforts on, because focus was essential. They knew from experience that trying to fix everything at once, means that you end up fixing nothing. Before we continue, let me now ask you; which of the three-areas identified would you focus on first, to begin improving the performance of Lego at that time?

- Expanding electronic toys?
- Reducing the number of business activities?
- Updating the supply chain?
- Other?

Lego management decided to zero-in on the supply chain issues. Why did they do that? Lego management did that because they soon realized that the outdated supply chain had been contributing to many the problems we just reviewed. For example, the outdated supply chain meant that Lego customer service was bad. In addition to that, product availability was horrible, due to the inefficient supply chain. Furthermore, Lego had designed their supply chain to serve very small retailers. However, in 2004 companies like Walmart, Carrefour and other big-box stores, were growing in importance for Lego. In addition to those issues, Lego management had been putting too much effort into brand-building, even though the Lego brand was already one of the most recognized brands in the world. Therefore, Lego management in 2004 decided to focus on fixing the supply chain first. This fix in fact included everything from product development, to sourcing, manufacturing and distribution.

Lego Operational Challenges

Let's now say something about each of the operational issues Lego faced. Regarding product development, new products at Lego was delivering less and less profit. Furthermore, only 30% of all Lego products generated 80% percent of sales. What this meant was that new product launches were not making a significant impact. On the matter of sourcing raw materials, Lego at the time had more than 11,000 suppliers (two times more than the aircraft manufacturer Boeing). This was a significant issue because that large supply network created a lot of complexity. In addition to this, Lego had very little negotiating power on contracts with suppliers, because of the fragmented supplier base.

Regarding manufacturing operations, Lego were using only70% of their production capacity, plus they had a very complicated manufacturing plant network, which was spread throughout many countries. Furthermore, the Lego distribution network had been designed to serve 1,000's of small toy shop retailers, even though 200 of their largest customers like Walmart (big-box retailers), represented 70%+ of the Lego business. Therefore, by focusing on re-engineering the supply chain, Lego were in fact able to address multiple challenges which the company was facing in 2004.

Because of these supply chain fixes, in just four years, CEO Jorgen Vig Knudstorp could regain Lego's profitability to more than two hundred million dollars, continue growth, and increase market share by +50%. The message for us all in this story is that effective and efficient supply chains are essential for any company who is faced with both stable and rapidly changing market conditions.

Best Practices

What are the best practices for a company's operations?

As we have emphasized throughout this Mini MBA, in today's fast changing business environment, one of the secrets for success is in fact to combine operational stability with operational-speed. That capability is like being able to write equally well with you left and right hand, which is called ambidextrous. Ambidextrous capability is quite uncommon; in fact, only 1% of people can naturally do that. Therefore, if only 1% of people are ambidextrous, you can imagine how rare it is for a company to be able to combine operational stability with operational-speed. Unfortunately for most companies, this capability is becoming increasingly important.

McKinsey & Co have been studying for the past decade management practices and their impact on organizational performance. One of the long-term McKinsey studies in this field is call the 'Company Health Index'.

That Health Index research has involved more than two million respondents, at over 1,000 companies worldwide. McKinsey update this Company Health Index research regularly. The categories which are measured in the Company Health Index fall into nine areas, of which innovation, coordination/control and capability, represent important operational topics. McKinsey have concluded from their Health Index research that companies who build both stability and speed into their operations have a +70% chance of being ranked in the top quartile of their Index. In other words, those companies outperform all other companies. In fact, those companies financially outperformed other companies by a considerable margin.

These McKinsey findings are also consistent with the research of Professor Rita Gunther McGrath (Columbia Business School). Prof. McGrath has investigated more than 2,300 large US companies over a ten-year period about agility.

What Prof. McGrath found was that only ten of those more than two thousand companies had increased their net income by a minimum of +5% annually during that ten-year period. The conclusion from that research was that those 10 high-performing companies were both extremely stable, meaning they had some structures that remained the same for a long period of time. However, when necessary they were also rapid innovators who could adjust and re-adjust their resources and operational capabilities very quickly. This ability to be both stable and dynamic is often referred to as operational agility. Being agile means that a company can have periods of stability, but when needed they can adapt quickly and easily to new challenges and opportunities, when they arise.

The Three Capabilities

The McKinsey's research also supported this idea of agility, because they identified three core capabilities in high performing companies that allowed those companies to become more agile. In other words, some unique capabilities allow them to effectively manage the tension between stability and flexibility. Those three agile capabilities were;

- **Organizational Structure:** Influences how resources are distributed in a company.
- **Governance:** Determines how decisions are made in a company.
- **Processes:** Decides how things get done, and influence performance measurement and accountability.

To understand in more depth what these three capabilities really mean, let's now say a few words about each. The first capability identified was agile structure. The research showed that the most successful companies often had one primary organizational structure which remained stable over time. However, those companies also had a secondary structure. The reason they had two structures was because the structures served very different purposes. The primary structure was critical as it created continuous stability in the organization. During this period of stability people in the organization understood those processes along with who they should regularly reported to. However, when more dynamic solutions were needed, the secondary structure was rapidly deployed.

Therefore, the primary structure supported continuity and stability (people like stability and certainty) and the secondary structure supported agility.

The second capability of high performing companies identified was agile governance. Agile governance means that within an organization, both stable and dynamic decision-making processes are used. A good example is when a company experiences very different conditions (a shift from a stable to a rapidly changing environment). During those conditions the organization must be able to quickly rotate individual members. However, under such conditions it is very important that member's roles and responsibilities are precisely defined beforehand.

The third capability of high performing companies identified by McKinsey had to do with agile processes. Agile processes mean that in addition to a company having rapidly forming teams when needed, they must have excellent stable core processes, and those stable core processes must be standardized, but still be hard for competitors to copy. Another unique element of an agile organization is that they must also put in place business-process owners. Business Process Owners are individuals who are primarily responsible for continuously improving those processes. In addition to Business Process Owners there is one additional critical role in agile organizations, and that role is the Integrator. The integrator in an agile organization is responsible for cross-functional collaboration (between sales, marketing, production, supply chain etc.), and is focused on continuously improving execution, performance management, meeting targets and more importantly, meeting KPI's. One could say that agile companies are unique in that they have developed these three capabilities, which help them to deal with both stability and change;

1. **Organizational Structure:** The primary and secondary structures influence how resources are distributed in a company.
2. **Governance:** Precisely defined roles and the rapid formation of teams determine how decisions are made under different conditions.
3. **Processes:** Process owners are selected, and integrators are appointed to manage cross functional collaboration and accountability under different conditions.

To determine your organizations current operational philosophy/capability, complete the STAB Assessment review. Place a check mark on each word (phrase which describes accurately your company's current practices). After that, add up the total number of checks for each quadrant (STAB). The result will reveal your company's primary operational philosophy. For example, if you have more checks in agile, your most likely philosophy is agile.

Once you have completed the analysis; consider what actions might need to be taken in to strengthen that primary capability or the actions needed to move into another operational philosophy (STAB).

STAB Assessment

Highest number of checks reveals primary operational philosophy

S = Startup	T = Trapped	A = Agile	B = Bureaucracy
❏ Startup	❏ Uncoordinated	❏ Quick to mobilize	❏ Risk-averse
❏ Chaotic	❏ Stuck	❏ Nimble	❏ Efficient
❏ Creative	❏ Empire building	❏ Collaborative	❏ Slow
❏ Frantic	❏ Fighting fires	❏ Easy to get things	❏ Bureaucratic
❏ Free-for-all	❏ Local tribes	done	❏ Standard way of
❏ Ad hoc	❏ Finger pointing	❏ Free flow of	working
❏ Reinvent wheel	❏ Under attack	information	❏ Siloes
❏ No boundaries	❏ Rigid	❏ Quick decision	❏ Decision
❏ Shifting focus	❏ Politics	making	escalation
❏ Unpredictable	❏ Protecting turf	❏ Empowered to	❏ Reliable
		act	❏ Centralized
		❏ Resilient	❏ Established
		❏ Learn from	
		failures	
TOTAL =	TOTAL =	TOTAL =	TOTAL =

S   T   A   B

DRILL 14: Summary

1. The waterfall metaphor represents the operations management approach best suited for stable conditions (finely tuned to optimize efficiency). The lake metaphor represents an agile operational philosophy. This flexibility, during less stable conditions, allows organizations to be more effective.

2. Operations management involves a wide range of activities including; supply chain management, logistics, production, quality, and distribution of goods and services.

3. It is important that some structures remain stable for a longer period. Agility means that when needed, a company's structure can adapt quickly and easily to new challenges and opportunities as they emerge. When those needs are solved, the organization can then rapidly return to the stable structure, governance and processes.

TASK: How Agile Are You?

The Maturity Index for Cultural Agility is developed by Vodaphone UK and Hewlett Packard. The score allows you to identify your level of Agility on the Agile maturity matrix.

- 0 – 80 points: Ad-hoc Agile
- 81-160 points: Doing Agile
- 161-240 points: Being Agile
- 241 – 320 points: Thinking Agile
- 320 points: Culturally Agile

LINK: Agile Maturity Assessment
https://goo.gl/rbHVZy
Note: Registration required for free assessment.

SOURCES:

Keith, O. et al. (2007). Rebuilding Lego, Brick by Brick. Booz and Company

Aghina, W. et al. (2015). Agility: it Rhymes with Stability. McKinsey Quarterly

Doeer, J. (2016). Insights from the Prophets and Practitioners. GOAL Summit, San Francisco

Bazigos, M. et al. (2015). Why Agility Pays. McKinsey Quarterly

Klau, R. (2013). How Google Sets Goals. Google Ventures

Gunther McGrath, R. (2013). The End of Competitive Advantage

DRILL 15: INTERNATIONAL

'Crystallized understanding of the most challenging environments' ~ Navy SEAL

A Small World?

When preparing this Mini MBA drill, I remembered the time many years ago when we brought the children to Disneyland. Disney had one ride during which you sat in a boat and floated through different tunnels. Each of the tunnels represented a different part of the world. In the background they were playing the same song repeatedly, and that song was; It's A Small World After All. Throughout that ride I was wondering; is it a small world after all?

The Amazon Marketplace MINI-CASE we will now discuss shows us that it might after all be a small world, and it's getting even smaller. This case is especially interesting for me because, when I first started in business it wasn't possible for almost anyone or any company, to become an international business overnight. So how can a company or even a person do that today through Amazon you might wonder?

CASE: Amazon Marketplaces

Online platforms like Amazon are massive and they cover almost the whole the world. For the moment at least Amazon.com are the largest internet-based retail platform in the world (but Chinese companies are catching up fast). Did you know that Amazon have an annual turnover of around $180 billion dollars, which makes them the #83 largest company in the Forbes Global 2000 list (the 3rd most valuable)? From 2006 to 2017 Amazon experienced an annual growth rate of +31% every year. Amazon operate eleven different online marketplace platforms around the world, and what this means is that Amazon have eleven countries where they can offer the complete service package. Customers in those eleven countries can get the product they want delivered in just a couple of days... if not in twenty-four hours. Of course, those marketplaces also deliver to neighboring countries, but the timing of deliveries etc. is then different. The eleven Amazon marketplace platforms (platforms were one of the three drivers of innovation) also enable sellers from anywhere in the world, to do business with the world. This can be done even though product standards and laws can differ on each market. Amazon also supports their sellers and helps them overcome all the normal international business challenges. As a matter of fact, Amazon provides almost all the services a company needs to become international immediately.

Amazon Service Portfolio

As an example of the Amazon portfolio of services, the Fulfillment by Amazon service (FBA) pick up your products, pack them, ship them to buyers, handle the buyers' online payments, and provide customer service (including product returns). Amazon can do all of that very effectively in more than eleven marketplaces. Amazon even offer twenty-four-hour customer service in local languages (Chū-I-wo-harau ...means pay attention in Japanese)! How is your Japanese? Another benefit of the Amazon marketplace is the large amount of data they collect about customer online buying behavior. One example of using this data is the Selling Coach Dashboard (SCD). SCD is a platform service which gives sellers information like; recommendations on products they can sell in other marketplaces. Warnings to restock their inventory (to avoid running out of stock or pre-fulfillment cancellation risks). Information on customers who have shown interest in a product, but that product might have limited availability, and therefore represents an opportunity for sellers if they have that product available. In addition, Amazon offer free shipping for Prime customers.

Amazon also has what they call the Match Low Price Feature. That feature informs a supplier when there are other products available at lower prices than what that supplier currently offers. In other words, Amazon can even help sellers make pricing decisions. In fact, with Amazon, all that a seller must do anywhere in the world is; have their product shipped to an Amazon fulfillment center, and from there Amazon does everything else.

Therefore, unlike when I first started in international business, any individual or company can get involved in international business with Amazon by merely;

- Having a product (can be outsourced from anywhere in the world).
- Have product sent to one of the Amazon fulfillment locations.
- Arrange banking services (to receive payments from Amazon).
- Organize tax payments with authorities.

The online marketplaces offered by Amazon, Alibaba, eBay and others have in fact made the world a small place after all! In todays connected world, international business is possible for almost anyone. Maybe Disney was right?

This all sounds very rosy, doesn't it? However, despite the rapid rise of online marketplaces, most of international trade which occurs today is not online, and still occurs in a more traditional way. In a previous Mini MBA drill, we said Amazon has only 4%+ of the total US retail market. What this means is that most of retail sales worldwide are still done in a more traditional way. As a matter of fact, most of international business is still also done in a more traditional way.

Now, let's drill-down deeper into those more traditional ways of doing international business. There are three important questions which every company, or individual for that matter, must consider before deciding to go international, and those three questions are;

1. WHY go international?
2. WHERE to go?
3. HOW to organize international business?

What Is International Business?

In a moment, we will drill-down deeper into the three questions listed above. However, before doing that lets consider a simple question; what is international business?

This is a challenging question because; international business can mean different things for different people. Therefore, it's important first to arrive at a common understanding of what we are talking about. Therefore, let's agree on a common definition. To do that, we could first think of some international business examples. Imagine that you have a company making bicycles and you buy some parts for those bicycles from an overseas country (bicycle chains). So, you buy chains, import them into your country and then you put them on your bicycles, and sell the bicycles in your home market. Is that international business for your company? I would say it is, because you're importing from overseas the chains, and that import activity, involves many of the traditional international business activities (identifying suppliers, negotiating with foreign sellers, shipping, and foreign currency transactions etc.

Forms of International Business

Here's another example, which better illustrates what we call, in-direct international business. Let's say that you have a company which is producing and selling a product to local customers (not importing any parts) within your home country, for example a door lock for cars. You sell the car door locks to a company in your country who are assembling the Mercedes-Benz GLC car for the German company Mercedes (yes... Mercedes use a sub-contractor to assemble the GLC). Anyway, that Mercedes GLC car lock is just a small part (value) of the complete car.

Now imagine what happens with that car. Mercedes exports the complete Mercedes-Benz GLC to Russia, for example. This mean that the Mercedes GLC in Russia will have your company's car door lock in it. Is that international business for your car lock company? Yes, it is, and that represents in-direct exporting. Another example of in-direct exports might be as follows; your company produces chocolate candy in your home country, you identify an independent export company in your country, and that export company exports and your chocolates to the United States. That would also represent in-direct exports for your chocolate company.

From these simple examples, we could now imagine more complicated cases such as; your company have their own sales office in a foreign country. Another example might be that you have a factory overseas, and that factory produces products for that foreign market, or you import into your home-market products which are produced in that overseas factory. Therefore, the process of becoming international can begin by simply importing something, move to a more in-direct export method (selling the car lock to a car assembly factory, who then exports the GLC to Russia). From there, more direct-export methods can be employed.

An example of direct-exports is when, your company exports directly a product you have produced in your home country to some distant foreign market. From there you might establish a sales office in another country, start producing products in your own factory overseas, and even start importing back into your home country the products you produce overseas. There might even be a case where your company will stop all production activities in your home country, and everything you sell in your home market is imported from the factory that you operate overseas. The conclusion we can draw from this is that there are many different forms and types of international business. Now that we have agreed about what international business involves (Inward, Outward, Collaborative, Foreign Direct Investments and more), let's return to the three questions we listed earlier;

1. WHY go international?
2. WHERE to go?
3. HOW to organize that international business?

Why Go International?

The first of these questions (WHY?) is probably the most important question of all, when discussing international business. However, to answer that question, we must first consider a few things. The first of those questions is; are we willing and capable to succeed in international business? After we have decided that, we should think a lot about the market opportunities; does one exist, what is it, how big is it, etc.? If we discover that there is willingness, but we lack some capabilities which are necessary to succeed, we then need to spend a lot of time thinking about the capabilities we need, and how to obtain them? For example, are those capabilities resources or knowhow? Let's now discuss some of these important issues one at a time.

First on our list is the; are we willing and able question. To answer that question, we must determine the level of commitment. This especially means that we must determine the level of commitment of senior leaders and managers in our company. This is essential because, it can take a long time, an awful lot of resources, and many failures before we succeed in our international business. If top management are not committed to this reality (rewards follow time, and risks), all that will result from the hard work will be an expensive failure. Being able also means we must determine; do we have the knowhow and necessary capabilities (product knowhow, market knowhow and capability/capacity to serve those markets)? Some other questions we might ask at this stage include;

- Does an opportunity really exist, and what is that opportunity?
- Is that opportunity big enough or attractive enough for us?
- How easy or hard will it be to realize that opportunity?
- What are the risks (short and long term), including the impact on our existing business and markets?

One important risk we should consider includes the effect of foreign currency exposure to our business. These questions might sound very serious and rather challenging however, the good news is that international business can be very rewarding. As an example of this, international business can bring with it the benefits of geographical diversification. For example, imagine that in your company, you can see that the home market is declining, and sales are dropping. Profitability is getting harder and harder to maintain, and the market might even be getting smaller due to lots of competitors, or a declining need for your product or service. Now imagine that out there, somewhere in the world, there are markets which are growing, and they are becoming increasingly attractive. If you decide to enter one of those growing markets, you are in fact geographically diversifying your business. By doing this, your company can balance (or reduce) the negative effects of declining home market sales. So, there is some good news here. Of course, you must remember that it will take time and money to enter that growing market, and to make it a profitable business for your company. However, despite this, there are considerable benefits to geographical diversification.

Resources and Knowhow

Another question we asked a moment ago was; if we are willing but not capable, what resources or knowhow do we need to develop or invest, which will increase our chances of success? This is in fact a very important question, because, if we find that our capabilities need to be improved. This could be done by developing or recruiting the necessary people, or identify more affordable resources which are necessary for us to succeed. However, here is an interesting point, those necessary resources or capabilities which we need, might also be available outside of our home country such as; knowhow, raw materials, parts, a finished product or component and more. Furthermore, they might even be available at a lower cost (labor and material costs are lower etc.). The important point here is that, those essential capabilities we identify abroad might also make it possible for business to continue being active on our home market. Therefore, a company can also benefit in their home market when they identify the capabilities and resources needed overseas.

As you can tell by now, there are many things to consider when deciding on the willing and able question. Many of those questions have a lot to do with existing markets, along with any foreign market a company might be considering. However, also keep in mind; this does not always have to do with market opportunities. Because it can also involve identify more competitive sources of raw materials, parts, knowhow etc. which are needed to remain competitive at home. Despite these different reasons for becoming international, the most important question to ask is; can we make more money by being involved in international business?

Spotlight on US Trade

If you are interested in making money, you might want to hear about a recent study made by HSBC Bank (a British-based bank and the 4th largest bank in the world). The research study is called HSBC 'Spotlight on US Trade'. In that research, HSBC investigated the profitability of the largest companies in the US Northeast. The findings revealed that the average profit margin for highly international companies in that region was 7.7%, over the five-year period examined. However, companies in the same region, who had low levels of international business, were unprofitable during that same period.

These HSBC findings illustrate the positive impact a geographically diversified market-base can have on the profitability of a business! Those highly international companies also had a stable upward trend in their average profit margins, while the profit margins for companies with low levels of international business in the Northeast were extremely volatile. Furthermore, highly international companies can insulate, or protect themselves, from US market uncertainty (fluctuations). The largest export country for the highly international companies was? Before revealing the answer, what do you think what was the biggest export country for companies studied in the HSBC research? Well the largest export country was Canada, which is right next door to the USA. In international business language we call this geographical proximity (close neighboring country). This is an important point to remember, and we will discuss this in more detail in just a moment however, first let's talk economics and world trade for a minute.

World Trade

When we look at world trade data, we can see that world exports alone represent a large part of international trade. Furthermore, world exports are growing faster than the economies of most individual countries. World trade today is growing annually at around +3.8% worldwide. That growth rate is higher than most of the major economies, or individual country growth rates. We can also see from the trade data that world trade (international business activities) is very important for some of the largest countries (even more important for small countries). For example, German exports represent almost 50% of the country's total economic output. For many small countries in the world, the percentage of the economy which is linked to international business activities is even higher. Therefore, international trade can offer market and growth opportunities. Furthermore, it can also represent a large part of a company's (if not a nations) total economic activity.

However, despite what might look like a rosy picture, every company must still consider; why do they want to be involved in international business and are they capable of succeeding (if not, what do they need to do to increase their capabilities)? For example, imagine that your company has a tiny share of your home market (1%-2%). Would it not be better for you to develop your home market further, before beginning to explore the foggy, unknown and risky international marketplace?

Where to Go?

The 2nd question we asked at the beginning of this Bootcamp drill was; where to go? The simple answer to this question is; start in a country which is close, familiar, and has similar business practices and needs. Let's now give some examples to illustrate this important point;

- The #1 export market for US companies is Canada, and the 3RD largest is Mexico.
- The largest trading partner for Germany is France.
- The United Kingdom is the 2nd largest export market for Ireland.
- Hong Kong and Japan are the 2nd and 3rd largest export markets for China.
- South Africa is the largest trading partner for Zimbabwe.
- China is the largest trading partner for India, and for Australia.

I think that you get the point here, right! Proximity (or being close to a trading partner) seems to make to make a lot of sense, and can have its benefits. However, that is a rather simplified answer, because the more complicated answer to this question would be; a company must do its homework, and that homework must involve a thorough analysis of individual markets and opportunities. Furthermore, for each individual potential foreign market being considered, the following things must be investigated;

- The real potential market size (for your business).
- The growth rate on that market.
- The market segments (different customer groups should be identified and understood).
- The specific customer needs and how those needs differ from what you are accustomed to today.
- The competition (who are they, what are their unique capabilities, what threat do they pose for you).

The market risk (currency exposure, political risks etc.).
Furthermore, one should also look at other factors (environmental conditions; cultural, legal, technological requirements etc.). The best way to answer these questions is to begin your homework by investigating and researching the potential on a range of international market. Following that, you, slowly narrow those down the options to the most attractive (based on your unique capabilities and the opportunities you identify). However, remember that there are over 200 countries in the world. Furthermore, it might be wise at the very beginning to follow the simple rule; start with a country that is close, familiar and has similar business practices and needs to your current business activities and customers. By

doing just that, your company can begin to learn about doing international business, and what is required to succeed. This might be a wise choice for first-time international companies because, the more you learn, the better prepared your company will be later to expand towards less known countries which are geographically farther and farther from your home market.

OLI Analysis

The final question we raised at the start of this drill was;

'How to organize the international business?'

There are two frameworks (tools) which can help determine the answer to that question. The first tool is called the OLI framework, and the second is called the IR Grid. By completing the OLI analysis, a company can determine what form of business (or operational mode) should be used on a specific target market (foreign country)? As an example of this, should the company license their product, or should they export (in-directly or directly). Or, the company might need to make a bigger commitment (direct investment) on the foreign market being considered (investing in a factory or distribution center etc.). In international business these choices are often referred to as the Mode of Operation. The mode best mode is normally determined by first analyzing a company's advantages and capabilities (OLI analysis) and for each foreign country being considered, a company might ask the following questions;

1. Do we have only an ownership advantage?
2. Do we have an ownership advantage and internalization advantage?
3. Do we have advantages in ownership, internalization and location?

Let's now say a few words about those three different advantages; ownership, internalization and location. Ownership advantage means a company has a specific competitive advantage over others, which makes it more likely that they can successfully do business on a specific foreign market. Those ownership advantages could be; superior brand, superior product, or other special capabilities.

Internalization advantage means that a company is better off carrying out activities on their own, because they have internal capabilities which are unique and give them some advantages over other companies they compete with. Those advantages could be production process knowhow, or unique systems and more. Location advantage, requires that a company have (on their home market) the necessary resources and knowhow (market knowhow, money, raw materials, low cost labor, tax advantages etc.) that are enough for them to compete successfully on the foreign market they are considering.

The more the immobile, natural or created resources, which firms need to use jointly with their own competitive advantages, favor a presence in a foreign location, the more firms will choose to augment or exploit their O specific advantages by engaging in FDI.

If a company determines that they don't have all the necessary advantages, then they might consider how to obtain those advantages. This could mean that they need to consider investing in a country they are considering entering. They may be necessary because, otherwise they might not succeed. Therefore, based on the OLI analysis, a company can see where they have advantages or disadvantages in;

- Ownership
- Internalization
- Location

If a company has advantages in all three OLI fields, they are in a strong position for making an investment directly in a target market (foreign direct investment). However, if they only have ownership and internal advantages, then it might be better for them to just consider exporting (indirectly or directly). Finally, if they only have ownership advantages, they would be better off sell a license, to someone who will do all the rest.

If a company has no advantages at all, they are not ready to risk getting involved in international businesses, unless they wish to learn. Furthermore, that learning could also help them to get stronger on their home market! However, learning takes time; it can be expensive and risky. The OLI framework is a very useful tool for any company who is considering international business, The OLI can be used to evaluate every single market or being considered. Moreover, OLI can help a company decide which operational mode would be best for them based on the ownership, internalization and location advantages they might possess.

The OLI Framework

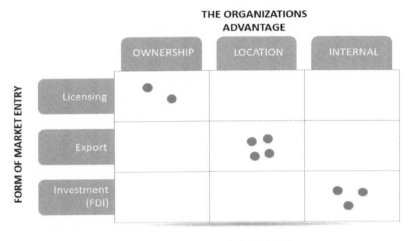

Source: Dunning 1981

The IR Grid

The second international strategy tool (IR Grid) is used to help a company, after they have decided what mode of operation is most suitable. This tool helps a company consider the level of integration and the level of responsiveness required on each target market being considered. Therefore, the IR Grid helps companies manage the two conflicting pressures they will, and which determined the level of efficiency and effectiveness on those markets.

Dunkin Donuts

Here's an interesting example of how the IR Grid can be used in a business. Dunkin Donuts are a US coffee and donuts chain, which was established in 1950. Dunkin sell more than fifty-two types of donuts and serve more than three million customers every day around the world. The company has more than 11,300 Dunkin Donut restaurants worldwide, and China is just one of the many foreign markets than Dunkin operate on. So, how might the IR grid help Dunkin? Well, Dunkin Donuts China realized quickly that they had to respond to local Chinese tastes by adapting their donut flavors for that market.

As an example of that adaptation, Dunkin today offers seaweed, sesame, and pork floss flavored donuts in China, which are flavors that most American customers would not find very appealing? The IR Grid helped Dunkin decide how responsive they needed to be on the Chinese market, for them to be effective on that market. Furthermore, the IR Grid analysis also helps Dunkin determine how integrated they need to be in China, to maintain efficiency in their operations.

Integration-Responsiveness Grid

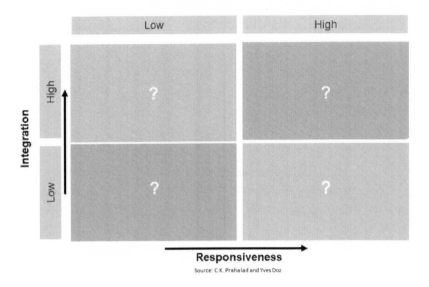

Source: C.K. Prahalad and Yves Doz

The Four Quadrants

Let's discuss each of the four quadrants in the IR grid and discuss some examples of companies in each of the four quadrants. The bottom left box in the IR Grid could be named international strategy. In this box we might have a company like Sekkingstad As, who are one of Norway's largest independent suppliers of Atlantic salmon. By the way...the country of Norway is the world's leading producer of Atlantic salmon and the second largest seafood exporter in the world. Well, we could say that Sekkingstad As Norway have a standard product (salmon), and in fact that product is generic (or common) all over the world. All Sekkingstad production and processing facilities are in Norway, and they are exporting most of their fish to other European countries. Therefore, Sekkingstad have a low level need to adapt their product on individual target markets and they keep their business centralized in Norway. In other words, their need for responsiveness is low.

In addition to this, Sekkingstad has standardized and centralized operations that given them high levels of control. In other words, they have a low-level need for global integration. Therefore, Sekkingstad Ab Norway would be a typical company who face low pressures for local responsiveness and low pressures for global integration, and in fact, an international strategy would best suit this company.

Now let's move to the bottom right box of the IR Grid. We can name this box; Multi-domestic Strategy. Companies who find themselves in this Multi-domestic box have a high level of pressure for local responsiveness, but a low level of pressure for global integration. Can you think of any companies that might fit into this Multi-domestic box? Well we might place Banco Santander retail banking (the 17th largest bank in the world) in this box. Banco Santander is a Spanish banking group who has expanded internationally by acquiring other banking companies. Santander is in fact the thirty seventh largest companies in the world today.

The reason we placed Santander retail banking in this box is because, their need for standardized and centralized control is useful, but not necessarily occurring across international operations. However, for Santander to be effective on local retail banking markets in different countries, they must adapt their activities (including some decentralization) and offer some customized products based on the needs of customers in each market they operate on. Therefore, Santander (retail banking) is a very good example of a multi-domestic strategy.

Now lest shift to the top left box of our IR grid. We can name this box Global Strategy. What do you think, what company might fit in this Global Strategy box? Well, a good example of a company that fits in this box is the Boeing Aircraft Company. Boeing is the world's leading manufacturer of commercial jetliners and is America's biggest manufacturing exporter.

In fact, Boeing exports to more than 150 countries around the world. So why did we place Boeing in the Global Strategy Box? Well, we placed Boeing there because, most of the Boeing aircraft sold around the world are standard, although there are some local needs to meet (interiors, seating, power plant etc.). However, a Boeing 737 (for which they have delivered more than 9,000 since they first started manufacturing them in n1965) is pretty much a standardized product produced in the USA.

By the way, a top-class Boeing 737-900 ER costs about one hundred million dollars new. The high level of standardization at Boeing means that they must have very centralized control across all international activities. Boeing does this to maintain control over technical standards, safety, quality and costs. Therefore, Boeing is a great example of a global strategy company.

Finally, we have the box on the top right of the IR Grid, and we can call this box Transnational Strategy. Can you think of any companies that might fit in there? Well, we could put Amazon Marketplace there. Amazon has their marketplaces in eleven different countries around the world and the product assortment offered on those markets can differ considerably. This is because Amazon must adapt their business model based on the needs of markets such as Japan, Mexico and China, because customers on those markets have different needs. Amazon needs to have a very high level of standardization in their platform throughout the world, along with centralized control of technology development. This means that Amazon is operating a transitional strategy.

The IR grid can help a company determine the best international strategy, but in addition to that, it can also help determine the best organization form for different markets. The IR grid analysis can also help a company understand better the need for changes in their strategy, and their positioning on markets over time. The IR grid can also help managers determine the level of threats or opportunities in their business, due to changes in cost structures, political pressures, and competitive conditions.

It's important to remember that companies can migrate from one strategy to another, as their international business develops and the need for responsiveness or integration grows in their business. In addition, the IR Grid analysis can also help managers to decide what changes might be needed at a business function level (manufacturing, finance, marketing and other functional areas).

DRILL 15: Summary

1. The primary reason companies explore international business opportunities is because they are seeking a market opportunity however, a company could also seek out resources and knowhow.
2. Most companies start their international activities in a country which is close, familiar and has similar business practices and needs, when compared to their home market.
3. Companies must always consider their advantages; ownership, internal and location, along with the needs for integration or local responsiveness on each foreign market being considered.

TASK: Are You Ready?

Take this Thunderbird School of Business and University of Hartford online test to determine if your company is ready for internationalization?

LINK: Are You Ready?
https://goo.gl/uwZnV1
Note: No registration is required for this assessment

SOURCES:

HSBC Spotlight on US Trade (2013)

Global Economic Data (2016). The Global Economy.org

Dunning, J. (1979). Towards an Eclectic Theory of Economic Production. Journal of International Business Studies

Prahlad, C.K., & Dos, Y. (1987). The Multinational Mission: Balancing Local Demands and Global Vision. The Free Press

DRILL 16: STRATEGY

"Don't run to your death" ~ Navy SEAL

Google the word strategy and you will get almost 740 million hits. There is no way we can cover such a complex topic in a few minutes therefore, in this Bootcamp drill we must focus-in on just one critical strategic topic. Choosing that one strategic topic could be exceptionally difficult. However, in this Bootcamp we will do that for you. The strategic topic we have chosen is in fact very important for every company, and for your future career. That strategic topic is; 'How to navigate a business through continuous change and disruption? To help answer this question, we will rely on the ideas of one of the leading expert in the field of strategy (Martin Reeves). Martin is a Senior Partner and Managing Director of The Boston Consulting Group's (BCG) New York City office.

In the beginning of this Bootcamp, we discussed change and how change has now become a permanent part of every business. We also discussed agility, along with the need to adapt, if we wish to survive and prosper in these fast-changing times. Martin Reeves argues that; the traditional approaches to company strategy do not fit these conditions. However, not all companies are faced with the same levels of change in their business environments. Furthermore, not all companies have the capabilities to influence the change which is occurring. The important point Martin makes is that; different strategies are required for different conditions.

Four Strategic Styles

BCG developed a framework which can be used to determine the best strategic style based on the environmental conditions a company might face (two different business environmental conditions). The framework reveals four different strategic styles suitable for those two conditions. BCG also came up with a 5th style, which we won't discuss in detail here.

That 5th style is called Survival. During survival, companies take a defensive posture, focused on radically reducing costs and business activities, to survive the crisis. They do this in the hope that the crisis will end soon, otherwise they are dead, because the clock is ticking fast when a company are not making the necessary investments in developing their business for the future.

As was said a moment ago, the strategic styles we will focus in-on this Bootcamp drill are based on two different business conditions. The first of those conditions is the level of predictability in the business environment. Predictability considers 'how far into the future and how accurately, a company can confidently forecast demand, performance, competition, and market expectations'. The second condition is called Malleability, let's use the word workable. Workable (or malleability in BCG lingo), defines to what extent a company or their competitors can... influence the predictability factors we just listed.

Based on these variables (predictability and malleability) one can then construct a four-quadrant strategic style matrix, and based on how predictable and how workable (or malleable) the environment is for a business a company can position their business on the BCG Strategic Style Matrix. Depending on which of the four quadrants a company fits into, one can also determine the best strategic planning method for that company. According to BCG research findings, companies who best match their strategy style with the conditions in their business environment; have been found to perform much better than others, who do not match style with environment.

Successfully matching strategic style with conditions in the market can result in an increase in returns of + 4% to +8%. The BCG Strategic Style Matrix has four quadrants.

Strategic Style

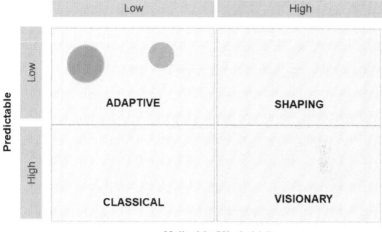

Source: BCG Analysis

Classical Style

The first quadrant is called the Classical Style. The classical style fits best predictable but hard to change environments. This means that a company can set goals. Target favorable markets, and benefit from its resources, capabilities and advantages. Furthermore, their strategies can be used for years in the future. Can you think of any examples of companies who might fit this style? The Shell oil company is in fact a good example of the classical style. This is because; Shell can act on long term and reliable forecasts of energy supplies and consumption patterns.

Adaptive Style

The second style is called Adaptive. The adaptive style is suitable in less predictable and faster moving conditions. However, companies using this style are is still capable of adapting to the conditions, when they make the right decisions. Can you think of any company examples of companies who might fit this style? Zara, the clothes retailer is a good example of the adaptive style. This is because, if Zara act properly, they can adapt to conditions as they are changing. In fact, new styles and fashion trends can be introduced within three weeks at Zara. Zara have highly effective design and manufacturing capabilities, unlike most other retailers who can take from four to eight weeks when adapting to those same conditions. In both the classical and adaptive style, companies like Shell and Zara are very capable of creating opportunities within given environmental conditions.

Shaping Style

The third BCG strategic style is called Shaping. According to Martin, Internet software companies often use this style. They do so because they are faced with an unpredictable future and one in which competitors are entering all the time. Furthermore, growth is very rapid in shaping environments; therefore, the goal for companies is try and shape the environment to obtain advantages, before another company does so. Flexibility is critical for the shaping style to succeed, because shaping style companies can't rely on accurate predictions of the future. Therefore, they must be experimenting all the time to discover solution to the highly unpredictable environment they operate within. Quite often shapers are also collaborating with other companies to reduce the risks of experimentation.

Visionary Style

The 4th and final style is Visionary. Visionary companies have both the power to shape the future of the industry, and they can predict the future. Often you can see visionary companies operating in entirely new markets. Under such conditions, they must be able to quickly assemble the necessary resources and execution is critical. Furthermore, having a lot of 'GRIT' can help! The visionary style could be viewed as a more entrepreneurial way of working. By the way, in the final drill of this Bootcamp we discuss startup and we will address more the challenges of having a visionary style.

The BCG Strategic Style Matrix research also discovered that the most common style used by companies today are most suited to predictable environments (40%use visionary and 35% classical, 16% adaptive and 9% shaping). This is especially interesting because, companies are using these styles, even if their environments are clearly unpredictable, and this is a big strategic mistake indeed!

DRILL 16: Summary

1. Two conditions in a company's business environment determine the best strategic style for that company. The first condition is the level of predictability and the second condition malleability.
2. There are four strategic styles which suit the above environments; classical, adaptive, shaping and visionary. The classical and adaptive styles are suitable for companies who can create opportunities within fixed environmental constraints. Shaping and visionary styles are suitable when the business environment can be shaped or molded (if a company has that capability).
3. Most companies use classical and visionary styles (75% of the time) even though they might be operating in unpredictable environments (a big strategic mistake).

To conclude this strategy session, you will be presented with two different assignment options. The first assignment will help you better understand what organizational issues need to be considered, when implementing a strategy within your current employer. The second assignment will allow you to complete one-of-two online cases (Boston Consulting Group). The online case assignment will give you a better understanding of how the business environment can impact strategy formulation.

TASK: Organizational DNA

To fully understand your companies' DNA, you would benefit from completing the three-step online DNA assessment below.

'There are only a few organizational personality types. Every company may seem unique, but in their enterprise-wide behavior, they fall into just seven behavioral patterns (in order from the least to most effective at strategy execution): passive-aggressive, over-managed, outgrown, fits-and-starts, just-in-time, military-precision, and resilient. That means that, no matter how challenging a performance problem may seem the solution may be achieved by changing the organizational personality.' ~ G.L. Nielson & J. Estupinan (2014) Strategy&

STEP 1: Organization Coherence Index

The Coherence Index specifically measures the coherence or consistency of your organization's strategy. Diagnose your organizations Coherence Index now. Please make a note of your findings, reflect on the Organization Coherence Index findings and what they may mean for your business, along with what actions are needed.

LINK: Organization Coherence Index Assessment
https://goo.gl/gwakkJ

STEP 2: Organization DNA Assessment

Faced with the same market, stocked with similar talent, one organization flourishes, while the other flounders. Organizational DNA—explains why? Determine your organization's current DNA state (Passive-Aggressive, Fits-and-Starts, Outgrown, Over-managed, Just-in-Time, Military Precision, or Resilient). Diagnose your organizations Coherence DNA now. Please make a note of your findings, reflect on the DNA findings and what they may mean for your business, along with what actions are needed.

LINK: DNA Profile Assessment
https://goo.gl/cFJt2K

STEP 3: Organization Effectiveness Assessment

'Consistent, coordinated, and controlled execution is the passport to sustained success in our global competitive environment', but how do you optimize execution? What actions would you take that you believe will most improve your organization's effectiveness (based on the DNA identified), over a one to two-year period. Each action will be calculated into execution building block impact. Reflect on the findings.

LINK: Organization Effectiveness Assessment
https://goo.gl/PsWy7E

BCG INTERACTIVE CASE

We challenge you to complete one of two Boston Consulting Group (BCG) online interactive cases. By completing the case, you will be able to practice what you have learned from this Strategy drill (strategic mindset). Before proceeding with the cases, please look at the short description below of the Harvard Case Method. This information will help you during the interactive case analysis.

Each BCG interactive online case will take 30+ minutes to complete. The results of decisions you make during the case are summarized at the end, and your case performance is compared to the historical average participants' performance. The following criteria are used by BCG to evaluate your case performance and decision-making capabilities;

- **Rigor**: Mathematical and analytical skills.
- **Business Judgement**: Ability to evaluate facts and consider risks and possible implications when deciding.
- **Structuring**: A logical approach to gathering and analyzing information.
- **Synthesis**: Bringing together all the information/analysis to decide.

LINK: BCG Case Library
https://goo.gl/wDxfHN

✓ **Airline Case:** Help the client (low-cost airline) remain profitable.
✓ **Drug Case:** Help the client (drug manufacturer) to set a suitable price.

Case Analysis Methodology
Harvard Business School

'A case study presents the greatest challenges confronting companies including; constraints and incomplete information. The case method places the student in the role of decision maker. There are no simple solutions to cases, however using case studies students can; become adept at analyzing issues, exercising judgement, and making difficult decisions.'

When completing the BCG interactive case above, the following analysis framework may help you to extract the maximum amount of value (learning) from the case experience.

1. **Defining the issue(s)**
   - What appears to be the problem(s)?
   - How do I know that these are problem?
   - What are the immediate issues that need to be addressed?
   - Differentiating between importance and urgency for the issues identified.

2. **Analyzing the data**
   - Why or how did these issues arise (resources, people, processes etc.)?
   - Who is affected most by these issues?

- What are the constraints and opportunities?
- What do the numbers (if any) tell you?
- Applying relevant Bootcamp: content, tools, and frameworks.

3. **Generating alternatives**
   - Being realistic!
   - Alternatives are mutually exclusive.
   - Doing nothing is an alternative.
   - Coming up with more than one decent alternative.
   - Support choices with relevant literature/sources (Bootcamp content).
   - Taking into consideration that alternatives need to be implemented.

4. **Selecting decision criteria**
   - How one decided which alternatives are best. For example: improve, increase, maintain, fits strategy, capability of implementing, risk, ease/speed of implementing, addresses employee issues, flexibility, impact etc.).
   - Employing some criteria in making choices/decisions (Bootcamp content).
   - Considering importance/impact to the organization.

5. **Analyzing/evaluating alternative solutions**
   - Measuring alternatives against key decision criteria.
   - Comparing alternatives to criteria and ranking.
   - Listing the advantages and disadvantages of alternatives.
   - Considering implications of each alternative.
   - Considering likely outcome of alternatives (best, worst, and most likely).

6. **Selecting preferred alternative(s)**
   - Process of decision making decision?
   - Consider if preferred alternative(s), resolve problem(s), along with your argumentation and logic.

7. Actions/implementation
- Drawing conclusions.

The case assessment rubric used in the Mini MBA Bootcamp leaders MBA courses is below. This rubric illustrates the generic assessment criteria for a MBA written case assignment.

CASE EVALUATION CRITERIA				
Evaluation Dimensions	Performance Rating			Score
	1 - 2	3 - 4	5 +	
Identification of Issues	Does not recognize the problems or issues of the case; displays little understanding of the issues	Identifies and outlines the principal problems and issues in the case; current situation, and strategic challenges	Accurate and detailed descriptions of the problems and issues, diagnosis, problems and strategic challenges	
Stakeholder Perspectives	Does not identify or explain the perspectives of any stakeholders involved in the case	Adequately identifies and summarizes the perspectives of the principal stakeholders involved in the case; conflicts of interest etc.	Describes the unique perspectives of multiple key stakeholders and insightful analysis of strategic tensions or conflicts of interest	
Connections to Theoretical and Empirical Research	Makes little or no connection between the issues and problems in the case and relevant theoretical and empirical research	Identifies and outlines connections between some issues and problems and relevant theoretical and empirical research	Insightful, and powerful connections between issues, theory and empirical data and integrates multiple sources of knowledge	
Analysis and Evaluation	Repeats facts identified in the case and not relevance, fails to draw conclusions and justification	Acceptable analysis of the issues and problems; in most instances, and adequately supported by theory and empirical data	Balanced, in-depth, and critical assessment of the facts of the case, insightful and well-supported conclusions	
Action Plans	Has difficulty identifying alternatives and appropriate courses of action	Outlines and summarizes some alternative courses of action; outlined, feasible, and based on relatively sound theory and evidence	Weighs and assesses a variety of alternative actions, proposes detailed plans of action; thorough and well-reasoned justifications	
Evaluation of Consequences	Displays limited awareness and/or understanding of the consequences of action plans	Demonstrates acceptable analysis of the results of proposed action plans; outlines, summarizes, considers courses of action, consequences of action	Objectively and critically reflects upon alternative plans of action; effectively identifies, discusses, and insightfully evaluates the implications and consequences of action plans	

Source: IACBE

Link: Case Evaluation Criteria (pdf)
https://goo.gl/bsnKDF

SOURCES:

Reeves, M. et al. (2012). Your Strategy Needs a Strategy. The Boston Consulting Group

Reeves, M., Love, C., & Tillmans, P. (2012). Your Strategy Needs a Strategy. Harvard Business Review

Reeves, M. (2015). Does Your Strategy Need a Strategy? Wharton, University of Pennsylvania

Gary, N., Martin, K.L. & Powers, E. (2008). The Secret to Successful Strategy Execution. Harvard Business Review

DRILL 17: CAREER

"What will the WIN look like when you get there?" ~ Navy SEAL

Can you guess what the number one predictor is of a successful match between two people who meet through an online dating site?

We will come back to this question in just a moment.

In this drill we will address the important topic of success in your career, along with the practical things that you can do to improve your chances of success. However, we should first all remember that being successful in a career can be the result of many things. For example, in an earlier Bootcamp drill we discussed the role GRIT plays in success.

We also talked about talent and skill, which also contribute to career success, although less significantly. During your working life you will have many career choices to make and making the right choices will at times be very difficult, and a very individual decision. Rather than discussing the large number of career choices you could make, and how you might succeed in each of those.

In this drill, the focus will be on the behavior that can make anyone a success in their career, no matter what that career choice might be.

Career Weapons

To understand better the behavior of successful people, we will use the research of Professor Robert Cialdini (Arizona State University). Prof. Cialdini has identified six career influence weapons which have been proven scientifically to help achieve success in many different types of careers. Learning more about these career weapons, and how and when to use them can benefit you in the future. However, before we talk about those six weapons, a word of warning. If you use these six weapons in an unethical or bad way, you may see some short-term wins in your career, but those short-term career wins will almost certainly be followed by long-term losses!

Reciprocity

Now let's discuss the Prof. Cialdini's six weapons. Weapon 1 is called reciprocity. To understand the power of reciprocity, I will first give a non-career example, and then we can discuss how this weapon might help you in your career. Imagine that you are in a food store, and as you are walking around the store you see a free food-tasting stand. Maybe the store is offering you a free tasting of a new product they are selling, and it might even be something you would really like to try. Most people are happy to get something for nothing, so you sample the new product (for free).

According to Prof. Cialdini, that experience of receiving something for nothing will in fact create a subconscious need or expectation for you to give something back in return. This expectation, to give something back, is very strong in people and will often lead them, at some point or another in the future, to offer something back in return. For the food store, this 'giving back' might mean that you buy the product you tasted, or you favor that store in the future. This behavior is called Reciprocity and the principle of reciprocity can also be applied in your career.

As an example of this, one of the most valuable assets you can give anyone in your work is to help another person to do their job better and become more successful. The best way you can do that is by giving them useful information. Giving information to someone first in fact, generates a feeling of gratitude in that other person; eventually causing those to want to reciprocate, in other words, give back to you. Here is another example of how to use the reciprocity weapon in your career. Imagine that you have just finished a job interview.

After the interview, you get home and you write a letter or email to the person who interviewed you. In that email you thank them for the interview, but you also pick out one thing about that company which the interviewer mentioned during your discussion. In your email, you describe some ideas you have about that matter, which you would like to share with the person who interviewed you, whenever they might be available to talk again. However (and this is the main point), in the email you also give them some of your thoughts on that matter, for example a solution to a problem they might be facing or an observation on another important matter the company might be facing. That email will make you stand out from all the other candidates, and that email is also a good example of the reciprocity weapon put into action. Professor Adam Grant (the Wharton School of Business) has also done considerable research on this behavior, and his research has shown that 'Givers' in the workplace or those who use reciprocity, often end up at the top of organizations.

Social Proof

The 2nd career weapon identified by Prof. Cialdini (Arizona State) is called Social Proof. This weapon is based on the principle that; when people are uncertain about a course of action, they tend to look to those around them to guide their decisions and actions, because they want to know what everyone else is doing, especially their peers. As an example of this, the next time you go into a fast-food restaurant like McDonalds, observe the other customers behavior. Why for example is everyone eating without forks, knives or chop sticks? Furthermore, why are they all bringing their garbage away, because that is not normal behavior in a restaurant, is it? That behavior you are observing is in fact based on the social proof weapon. The principle of social proof says that; we are more likely to do something if we see that many other people, who are like us, have also done it (for example eating with their fingers, and bringing the garbage away). This social proof weapon can also be effectively applied in your career.

For example, in business people like other people who are like themselves? Similarity might reflect itself in; behavior, opinions, personality traits, background, or life-styles. The best way to make your similarities familiar to another person you may wish to influence, is to have frequent, and pleasant contacts with that person. Frequent experiences mean that you have a have a much stronger and positive knowledge about each other. That familiarity in fact, establishes a level of comfort and a history between people.

Furthermore, if you complement other people, or praise them for their behavior (opinions etc.), they are more likely than not to accept those complements. This kind of behavior describes the social validation weapon. Social proof can also be applied in your career. For example, people prefer to say yes to requests from people they know and like. Therefore, by creating frequent and pleasant contacts with the necessary colleagues you wish to influence, you can help them to have a much stronger and positive knowledge about you, and you about them. This familiarity will in fact create a level of comfort and history. This means that they will be more likely in the future to say yes to a request from you and you from them. This is how social proof works.

Commitment + Consistency

The 3rd career weapon is called Commitment + Consistency. At the beginning of this drill we asked; what is the number one predictor of a successful match between two people on an online dating site. Well, according to the founder of OkCupid, one of the largest online dating sites in the USA, the number one predictor after connecting on OkCupid is a person's political beliefs or affiliation. In other words, if you are a Democrat and you date a Republican, you are much less likely to have a successful relationship, when compared to two democrats who connect through OkCupid.

Of course, it will matter how attractive the photo is of a candidate, and the personal profile will influence a person's choice for a first date. However, a much better predictor of a successful connection is a person's political beliefs (because we are very committed to those beliefs). This is an example the commitment principle, which we even can observe in online dating.

The commitment weapon can also be applied effectively in your career. For example, when you are next asked to attend a job interview, during that interview (preferably at the beginning), try to get the interviewer to say something positive about you. One way to get them to do that is by saying the following;

"I'm very pleased to be here today and happy to give you information about myself but, could I first ask, why did you decide to invite me for this interview?"

Just because you asked that question, the interviewer will most likely begin to explain the favorable features about you they identified with. Then, he or she will spend the rest of the interview time seeking to validate (demonstrate commitment) what they have publicly said about you! Another example of the Commitment + Consistency weapon can be very useful whenever you might be responsible for running meetings. This example is based on the principle that, when people leave a meeting without agreeing to a course of action, action is less is likely to happen. If, however each person at the end is asked to state their commitments out loud (what needs to be done next and by whom), that 'public' commitment to action is much more likely to happen.

Consistency is also very important for this career weapon to be effective. This is because people who are consistent are considered more trustworthy by others, and this leads other people to support them more. People also have a natural desire to stick to what they have said or agreed to at an earlier time, because we like to keep our promises, and that is being consistent.

The commitment + consistency weapon principle says that; people do not like to back out of commitments, and they try to be consistent with those commitments. This is the reason why when you asked the interviewer to state why they ask you for the interview, because of that question (and answer they gave), they almost must stick to that commitment during and even after the interview.

Liking

The fourth weapon is called Liking. This weapon is based on the principle that; people prefer to say 'yes 'to those they know and like. Furthermore, people are also more likely to favor those who are like themselves, or who give them compliments, because everyone likes a compliment. Just by making the effort to become more familiar with another person, can make them like you more. The key to liking is to be genuine and to ask questions of the other person. By doing this you always have something to come back to later in conversations with them. As a matter of fact, in your career there is perhaps no better influence than being liked. However, remember that being liked is closely associated with being trusted.

One-way people can exploit or take advantage of this liking weapon, is when they purposely find ways to make themselves more like another person. Be careful about exploiting this weapon, as it can backfire on you! In the workplace, people also tend to like others who appear to have similar opinions, personality traits, backgrounds, or lifestyles. As a matter of fact, the more like others you appear to be, the more likely they are to like you. According to Prof. Cialdini, most people also like flattery (or praise), even when they know it isn't true. People also like and trust anything familiar. Therefore, one of the best ways to build familiarity with those you wish to influence is to have frequent and pleasant contacts with them (frequency is more important than the amount on time spent during each contact). Familiarity often occurs after you have established a comfort level and a history with others.

Authority

The 5th weapon is called Authority. This weapon can also be applied effectively in your career. It can be applied effectively because throughout the world, most people are raised with a great respect for authority (real, implied and unspoken). Therefore, it is important to make sure...... that others know that your education and experience supports your ideas. Authority can also be demonstrated by the way you dress (like the people who are already in positions of authority that you seek).

True authority, is mostly noticed through behavior that is natural and constant. Body language for example, tone of voice, lack of insecurity, and composure are behavioral traits which demonstrate authority. According to Prof. Cialdini, just by acting assertive or by starting to lead others, you will see that people will have the urge to follow you. This happens because; most people are actively seeking out authority to follow. This is because, in the absence of authority or leadership, people become unsure of what to do. Therefore, those who act with a natural authority, dress for the role, and exhibit certain types of behavior are seen to have authority. That behavior might include;

- Minimal body movements.
- Stillness in the head.
- Direct attitude.
- Direct eye-contact.
- Taking up a lot of space (the dominant position).
- Assuming a high-status posture (Alexander Technique).
- Effortlessness facial expression.

Power-Posing

Professor Amy Cuddy (Harvard Business School) has done considerable research on 'Power Posing' and how our body posture influences others. Her research has shown that by practicing a power pose (standing tall with your hands stretched high above your head) for just two minutes, your testosterone levels (confidence hormone) increase by more than 20%, and cortisol levels (stress hormone) decrease by the same level. In other words, in just two minutes you can alter your perceived level of authority by others. However, one should always remember not to be too overconfident, because overconfidence can be dangerous in decision making and being genuine is usually appreciated more.

Video Link: Power Posing Video (Prof. A. Cuddy, Harvard)
https://goo.gl/eZf9GS

Scarcity

The 6th weapon is called Scarcity. This weapon is based on the principal that; opportunities seem more valuable when they are less available, or hard-to-get things are perceived as better than easy-to-get things. Scarcity means that there is a shortage of something, and in human psychology the possibility of losing something is a much more powerful motivator than that of gaining something. This is because limited resources and time limits increase the perceived value or benefits of everything, including your available time to help others, or their available time to help you. In your career situation, also try to let significant others know how valuable their scarce time or attention is valued by you; along with communication what they might miss, if they don't cooperate with you.

The principle of scarcity states that; things that are less available or less accessible become more attractive. Now maybe you might think that early on in your career you lack power and because of that you cannot use the scarcity weapon. Well in fact that is not true, you can! As an example of this, the next time you have a suggestion to make to your boss about something which might solve a problem for them, politely suggest a time for a meeting to discuss the matter and then add the following statement 'if your schedule allows for that'. Just by adding those six words to the discussion, 'if your schedule allows for that' you have confirmed the value and scarcity of that person's time.

These six career influence weapons can be incredibly powerful, and they can be combined in many ways. You can use the six weapons whenever you approach people who you want to influence. However, don't overuse the weapons and don't use them in an unethical way, because if you do… something bad might happen instead. In addition to this, please remember that according to the success formula covered in our very first Bootcamp drill. Success is; 2x more about 'GRIT', than talent or skill (including the skill of influencing others).

TASK: Are You an Influence Genius?

If you would like to test your capabilities in the six weapons, and to see if you are already an 'influence genius', Dr. Cialdine has created a short quiz which you can take online.

Link: Test Your Influence at Work
https://goo.gl/89Issz
Note: You must register before completing the assessment

SOURCES:

Cialdini, R. (1984) Influence: The Psychology of Persuasion.

Cialdini, R. (2016). Persuasion: A New Revolutionary Way to Influence and Persuade.

DRILL 18: Start-up

'Move, shoot, communicate' ~ Navy SEAL

Which of the following is the #1 reason startups fail?

1. Lack of market need
2. The team
3. Timing

In this final drill of the Bootcamp we will focus on the topic of startup failure (and we will answer the above question). According to the US Small Business Administration (SBA), 34% of small businesses fail in first two years, and 50% fail in first five years. Therefore, it seems that failure is more common that success in startups. In this drill we will focus on startup failure, and we will consider how to avoid the most common causes of failure. At the end of the drill we will also review the five reasons why most startups succeed.

S.T.O.P.P and Start-up Failure

Because of the 'failure' focus we are taking during this drill, we don't have time to discuss deeply the 'should I leap' question (should I begin). The should I leap question begins by considering whether you are the entrepreneurial type, and what might be driving your desire to start a business, for example; passion, over-confidence, an objective assessment of the situation, quality of idea, or personal circumstances. Before we go deeper into the causes of failure, here's a bit of trivia you might be interested in. Based on Harvard Business School data; 'entrepreneurs will earn 35% less in personal income over a 10-year period, compared to what they could have earned in a paid job.' After a person answers the 'should I leap question', and begins, the risks of failure grow and 90% of startups experience those risks.

I have been waiting patiently throughout this Bootcamp for an opportunity to introduce the UK Special Air Services (SAS) training drill for soldiers who find themselves in enemy territory.

That drill is called STOPP. And it can also be an effective tool for startups. STOPP stands for:

S = Stop
T = Think
O = Observe
P = Plan
P = Proceed

To understand better how the STOPP survival drill works; Imagine for a moment that you are a SAS soldier, and during the middle of the night you have parachuted into enemy territory. You are all alone, the enemy is not far away, and time is not on your side. However, all your SAS training has taught you that the worst thing you could do just then, is to immediately act and start moving. What your training did teach you is that you should;

Stop, **Think** about the situation, **Observe** the conditions around you, **Plan** for how you will deal with those conditions, and only then **Proceed** (act) on that plan.

In the startup world the STOPP Survival drill can also be applied, unfortunately though in a startup, you will find yourself in a different enemy territory every day. Some of those hostile territories you find yourself in will even be created yourself. For example; the decision you make when choosing your founding partners, and others hostile conditions will be coming from the market and from the competition. Therefore, as a startup founder, whenever you encounter these hostile conditions, you would be wise to remember the STOPP drill.

Reasons for Failure

The question then is; what are those hostile conditions which most frequently cause startups to fail? As you can imagine, there are multiple causes of startup failure and one could even argue that every case is different. However, on as general level, the causes of startup failure have been researched a lot, and in this drill, we will focus on the ten most common causes of failure. However, first a word of caution; remember that every startup is as unique as a snowflake, there are multiple things which might cause failure, and those things often occur at the same time. Furthermore, the decisions taken by founders at an early stage of development can be the root-cause of failure at a later stage (skills and capabilities of people chosen to be in the founding team).

The 10 causes of startup failure (landmines) we will now review have been identified by CBInsights.

#1 No Market

The #1 reason for failure was lack of market need (42% of the cases). In startup language this could be called lack of market validation (proof). If you remember anything from this drill, please remember that validation of the market demand for a startups product or service is more important than anything else! To help remember this, apply the STOPP Drill. You have landed in enemy startup territory. The first thing you must do is STOP and breathe deep. Then and only then, you Think about the situation you are facing (you must validate your idea).

After thinking a lot about this, you begin to observe what is going on; observe the market, enemies, allies and potential customers? What you need to determine from them is and understanding of the biggest problem your idea might solve for them. In other words, what is the biggest pain, they suffering because of that problem they face, and how are they currently dealing with that pain today (the present cure)? Then you plan, you plan how to validate your idea and how you can confirm that yours is the best medicine? And finally, you proceed, you move forward, you meet the allies and you do everything you can to understand their real pain, and how your idea might best cure that pain. That is how STOPP can help! However, it seems that often, startup founders fail to take these steps seriously, and that is why 42% of startups say that lack of market need for their product or service was the cause of their failure. Without market validation, the startup ends up with a product that no one will pay for. They burn a lot of time, energy, and cash and probably end up; stressed, depressed, or burned out. Furthermore, this process of validation can take two to three times longer than most founders thought it would. Please remember that!

#2 Money

The #2 reason for failure was money (29% of cases). In an earlier Bootcamp drill we discussed cash flow and how important it is to a business. Therefore, one of the most important jobs of a startup CEO/founder is to understand how much cash is available, and if that is enough to carry them to the next milestone (funding round). This is important because, meeting that milestone might result in the startup getting more financing. Unfortunately, many startups fail to reach that milestone, because they run out of cash too early. Therefore, the CEO/founders must carefully regulate the cash 'burn rate' in the early days, cash must be used conservatory.

Hiring too many people for example (sales and marketing staff), when the startup is still in the process of making a product that meets the market need (validation), is a common mistake. This is because, by hiring more people than is necessary, all you do in a startup is increase the cash burn rate, before the business model has even been proven. Or to put this another way, the startup must maintain a low burn rate, before the data is available that proves the cost to acquire a customer (CAC), is 3x lower, over a period of 12 months, than the revenue you can generate from that customer. Lack of cash should never be the reason for the failure of a validated idea, which has a financially viable business model!

#3 Founding Team

The #3 reason for failure was the founding team (23% of cases). It's unfortunate but true, if entrepreneurship is a battle, most casualties stem from friendly fire or self-inflicted wounds. The rule here is simple. The startup should have a balanced team with at least one technical founder and one business founder. Successful startups with just one founder in fact, have a much lower probability of growing their success, and if they manage to do even that, it will still take 3.5x times longer to achieve a scalable success level. Furthermore, founding teams as opposed to single founders will raise 30% more money and experience almost 3x more user growth!

#4 Competition

The #4 reason for failure was competition (19% of cases). A fact of life in today's business environment is that everything you build will be instantly copied. Therefore, the main challenge is to gain customers and keep them (retention). Please remember also that retaining customers is much easier (and less costly), than growing them or acquiring them. Therefore, startup founders should be focused on their existing customers, and while caring for those customers they are slowly building a brand that will withstand the competition. If a startup follows this rule, but still observes that they are losing customers to competitors, then some of the earlier issues we discussed might be the root-cause of the problem, rather than the competition. If a startup can't retain customers, they have a much bigger problem than just the competition.

#5 Price/Costs

The #5 reason for failure was with price & cost issues (18% of cases). The price for the product or service offered by a startup pays for the costs, so let's concentrate here on pricing. According to Sequoia Capital, a leading Silicon Valley venture capital company, Pricing is as much an art, as it is a science. Pricing also relies as much on marketing and psychology, as it does on classical economics. Therefore, setting the price is one of the most important decisions a startup can make. According to Professor Michael Dearing (Stanford University), pricing is not a math problem; in fact, it's a judgment problem. Dearing says that rather than focusing on the cost of their product, startups should think deeply about the value. To emphasize this point, Dearing often asks, 'why do most people think if they pay $50 for a bottle of wine, it's a better wine?

Offering variations of a product is one way to address the different values customers might have for that product. However, always remember that too many choices can often confuse customers. Therefore, when determining a pricing strategy, the startup would benefit much more from evaluating what might go through the customers mind when they are making the purchasing decision, and how different price-points might impact that final decision. In other words, STOPP!

#6 Poor Product

The #6 reason for failure was poor product (17% of cases). Poor product is often caused by a failure to establish the right product/market fit. In addition, often, the first product that a startup brings to market, does not meet the needs of the market. Therefore, in most cases, multiples changes are needed to get the right product/market fit. Furthermore, in most startups, the team does not do enough homework and they don't validate the idea with real customers (get out of the office).

#7 Business Model

The #7 reason failure was lack of a business model (17% of cases). Unfortunately, it is not uncommon for most startup founders to make the false assumption that customers will 'knock down the door' to buy their product. However, that is rarely the case. This is because, often, it is very, very and very expensive to attract and retain customers. Therefore, sooner rather than later, startup founders will discover that the Cost of Acquiring a Customer (CAC) is higher than the lifetime value (LTV) of that customer. The startup business model defines how a startup will, even at scale, acquire customers. And the business model defines how the startup will produce (monetize) those customers at a higher level than the CAC (Cost of Acquiring Customer). Under ideal conditions, the startup should be able to recover the CAC in less than 12 months. However, every founder should remember that 'ideas are cheap, but execution is dear'. What this means is that successfully executing the business model is as important as having the right business model in the first place.

#8 Marketing

The #8 reason for failure was poor marketing (14% of cases). The traditional marketing model (often referred to as the funnel) is based on making people want to buy your product. Traditionally, marketers achieve this by creating awareness, interest, desire, and eventually someone purchases the product. Unfortunately, that funnel model is costly, slow and can be ineffective. Therefore, many successful startups have found the use of guerrilla marketing tactics to be not only effective, but also cost-effective. However, guerrilla marketing requires creativity, flexibility and a willingness to take a risk. Furthermore, guerrilla marketing should not mean that the startup neglects existing customer follow-up and support.

Guerrilla marketing involves using the new emerging media channels, such as online and social and when this is done effectively it can result in a buzz being built around the brand or product being marketed. Often the result of guerrilla marketing is a memorable experience for customers. The impact of guerrilla marketing can be seen when people tell their friends about the experience, and through this word-of-mouse, the product or service concept reaches a lot more people. However, rather than talk on and on about guerrilla marketing, it might help to describe some case examples.

Case Example 1:

The Dollar Shave Club was started in 2011 as a mail-order razor blade business, which is not exactly sexy or rocket science. Customers paid one dollar a month to receive a quality product (Razor-2-Door). The guerilla marketing element in the business was that the company got a lot of consumer attention through a unique low-budget YouTube video. In 2016 the Dollar Shave Club was sold to Unilever Corporation for $1 Billion.

Case Example 2:

The Ice Bucket Challenge was started in 2014, and is another example of guerrilla marketing. The challenge started without any official charity and Chris Kennedy, a golfer in the USA, nominated the ALS Foundation as the recipient of the money raised. Kennedy posted her video on YouTube and from there, that peer-to-peer campaign raised an insane amount of money ($115 million). Now it's difficult to find a person who doesn't know about the disease ALS (motor neuron disease).

Case Example 3:

Tinder online dating app (founded in 2012), personally invited friends to download the app. They then visited the best "party colleges" and got attractive, influential figures to promote the app. Today Tinder has 26 million matches on their site every day.

I hope you get the idea however, remember that guerrilla marketing must involve some of the following ingredients;

- Should have a hook to get people's attention.
- Should be provocative (some controversy surrounding the message).
- Should sell an idea, not a product, because it's about emotional appeal and passion.
- Should be tangible (a real an object).
- Should involve some risk.

#9 Ignore Customer

The #9 reason for failure was ignoring the customer (14% of cases). The simple message here is; don't ignore your customers. The customer may not always know what is best for them, but you should never ignore them. The key to understanding your customers' needs is by 'walking in their shoes'. When Airbnb employees travel, guess where they stay, in Airbnb's. Even the founders of Airbnb have their homes listed on Airbnb. Analyzing data on customer behavior can also be exceptionally useful, and a great way to get to know your customers.

As an example of this power, Amazon also effectively uses that information to encourage people to buy. It's not an accident that they always tell buyers what other people are buying. Another effective way to gaining customer insights is by asking customers smart questions, which is much harder than you might imagine. When was the last time a company asked you a smart question (how likely is it that you would recommend our company to a colleague or friend, and why?). Finally, testing and learning is crucial for understanding customers. One way for the founders to test is by working on the customer service desk. Having the capability to learn quicker than everyone else and adapting the startup strategy based on what has been learned, may after all be the real secret to startup success.

#10 Timing

The #10 reason for startup failure was timing (13% of cases). In Silicon Valley there is a saying, which illustrates this point very well; too early, too early, and too late! What this means is that startup founders may have a great idea however, if the market isn't ready for that idea, they won't get anywhere. This is because the idea is presented to customers too early and frequently it is too late. According to Bill Gross (CEO, IdeaLab), timing is mostly about luck however, other factors do also come into play. Often, timing can be wrong due to economic conditions, but at other times technology might be the barrier.

Technology might be the barrier because people are not willing or able to adopt the technology, or some alternative technology emerges at the same time. However, economic conditions can also be the reason for perfect timing. As an example of this, when Airbnb launched their online apartment rental business, the US economy was entering a recession. But those economic conditions in fact created a positive reason to rent out ones' apartment to people (extra income). Furthermore, it represented a more affordable option for those people looking for a place to stay.

Therefore, carefully evaluating the signals in the market, is one way to understand the market, and might help to avoid the 'too early, too early, too late' timing challenge. However, this means that every startup must do their homework; understand the market conditions and the timing in their individual marketplace. When the startup does its homework, and understands these critical timing factors, they in fact have an advantage, even over larger competitors. They have an advantage because startups can be faster and more flexible in adapting to those market conditions which are influenced by timing.

To say this another way; the startup can pick the perfect time and execute much faster than larger and more established companies, who may take months, if not years, in adapting to rapidly changing market conditions. 'Too early, to early, too late', does not have to be the reason for a startups failure, if they do their homework.

STARTUP FAILURE

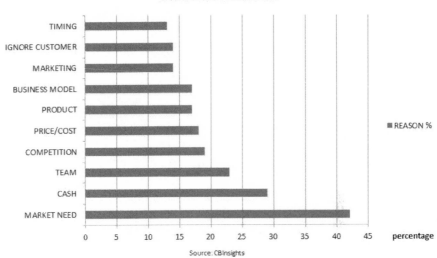

Source: CBInsights

Start-up Success

Now it's time to list the five reasons for startup success. Bill Gross (CEO, IdeaLab) has studied over 200 startups to try and determine what has been the reason for their success. From that research, Bill identified five critical factors for success (% of respondents);

1. 42% Timing (10th on list of failures).
2. 32% The Team (3rd on list of failures).
3. 28% Idea.
4. 24% Business Model.
5. 14% Funding.

The total adds up to more than 100% because in many cases there were multiples causes of success. Therefore, the #1 reason for startup success discovered by Bill Gross (IdeaLab) was timing, and the #1 reason for startup failure (CBInsights) was a lack of market need (validation). Based on this data, we could combine the findings from both studies and conclude that; the number one reason for success or failure in a startup is;

'Determining the right time for launch, which meets the needs of the market'

TASK: Have What It Takes?

Entrepreneur magazine have combined some of the most important element of successful entrepreneurs into a short test.

Link: Have What It Takes?
https://goo.gl/zMYSv3
Note: No registration is required to complete assessment

SOURCES:

Ghosh, S. (2011). Why Companies Fail: and How Their Founders Can Bounce Back. Working Knowledge, Harvard Business School

The Top 20 Reasons Startups Fail (2014). CBInsights

Gross, B. (2013). Lessons Learned from Bill Gross' 35 IPO's/Exits and 40 Failures, First Round Review

Final Mini MBA Assessment

'No institution can possibly survive if it needs geniuses or supermen/superwomen to manage it. It must be organized in such a way as to be able to get along under a leadership composed of average human beings'. ~ Peter Drucker

The Mini MBA Bootcamp has covered a broad range of management topics which a very relevant for every existing and future manager. To reinforce you're learning from the Mini MBA Bootcamp, we recommend that you now complete the final online assessment.

Link: Mini MBA Final Assessment
https://goo.gl/LRu29D

Good Luck

Thank you for completing the Mini MBA Bootcamp. Please now write a review in order that others can benefit from this book and increase their probability of success in business.

Amazon.com Review Page
https://goo.gl/VkQeJe

Kind regards
PAX
Dr. Gerard L. Danford

Other Kindle Books by Dr. Gerard Danford

Let's Talk About Business Strategy:

'95% of a company's employees are unaware of, or do not understand, its strategy'. Furthermore, companies on average deliver only 63% of the financial performance their strategies promise. Poorly communicated strategy is a major contributor to this performance loss. Without strategic clarity, nobody in the organization can help put in place a winning strategy!

Let's Talk About Strategy Link: Amazon.com
https://goo.gl/yy2EWa

Let's Talk About Strategy Link: Amazon.uk
https://goo.gl/yD2TuA